Hours

VOLUME I — THE EGYPTIAN PASSAGE

A Theology of Day and Night

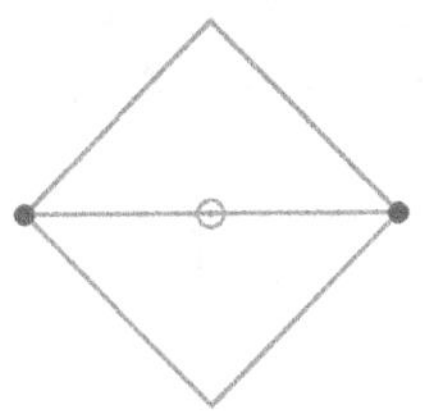

Kristi Hall

GRIST

Hours is being written as a four-volume work. Volume I, *The Egyptian Passage*, is published first. Volumes II through IV — *Nyx's Household*, *The Otherworld*, and *Helios* — are forthcoming.

Contents

Hours is a theology of the daily passage.

It is being written as a four-volume work. Volume I — what you are reading now — establishes the foundational claim and follows it into the Egyptian frame in particular: the twelve Hours of the Duat, the territory the night actually crosses, the figures who do the work of the passage. Volumes II through IV will take up the Greek night-deities, the Celtic festival cycle and otherworld, and the solar arc of the living hours, each in the same depth. Together they will make a complete account of what the night does and what the day produces, across the traditions that looked most carefully. Each volume stands on its own.

The first eight chapters establish what a day actually is — a complete cosmological cycle, structured by death and return, inhabited and mapped by the traditions that looked at it most carefully. The four chapters that follow open the Egyptian frame more fully, establishing the vessel, the crew, and the defenders of the night barque, and locating the practitioner within the image. The final twelve chapters move through the Hours of the Duat themselves — the territory the passage actually crosses, hour by hour, from the western mountain at dusk to the eastern horizon at dawn.

The book is meant to be read in order. The chapters build on each other, and the deeper material would not land without the foundation the earlier chapters lay.

A day is a passage. You are already inside one.

The only question is whether you cross it awake.

PART I

The Foundational Claim

I

What a Day Actually Is

A day is a passage. You are already inside one.

What is a day?

Not what it contains. Not what you do with it. Not how you feel at the end of it. What it *is* — structurally, cosmologically, as a fact of existence rather than a unit of measurement.

Most people have never been asked this question seriously. The answer feels obvious: a day is twenty-four hours. Sunrise to sunrise, or midnight to midnight if you prefer the civil version. A container of time, neutral in itself, filled with whatever you bring to it. This is the modern inheritance — secular, mechanical, and almost entirely without theology.

It is also, by the standards of every culture that looked carefully, wrong.

Not wrong about the hours. The mathematics of rotation are not in dispute. What is wrong is the assumption underneath the measurement — that a day is a container rather than a passage, a unit rather than a structure, something you move *through* rather than something that moves *you*.

Every tradition that looked carefully at a day saw the same thing. They saw a cycle with a specific shape. They saw a beginning that was not morning. They saw a death and a rebirth happening on a schedule so reliable that entire theologies were built to describe it. They saw, in other words, what we have mostly stopped seeing — that a day is a cosmological event, and that you are inside it whether you understand it or not.

The Celtic day begins at sundown.

That single fact is worth sitting with. Not as a curiosity of ancient timekeeping, but as a theological claim about the nature of reality. If the day begins in darkness, then darkness is not the end of something. It is the origin. Everything that follows — the long hours of night, the crossing into sleep, the return to waking, the full presence of the living hours — all of it emerges from darkness as its source.

Morning, in this framework, is not where a day starts. It is what a day has been working toward all night.

The Celts structured their festivals, their sacred calendar, their understanding of time itself around this principle. Samhain begins at sundown. So does every other sabbat on the Wheel. The darkness is not residual. It is generative. It comes first because it is first — not chronologically but ontologically. Night is the ground from which day is made.

The Egyptians arrived at the same truth from a different direction. Ra does not sleep. He travels. Each night the solar barque moves through the twelve hours of the Duat — the underworld, the deep structure beneath the visible world — navigating gates, meeting guardians, passing through transformations that are not metaphorical but literal in Egyptian cosmological thinking. At the end of that passage, Ra is reborn. The sun rises not because a celestial body has completed its rotation but because a deity has survived a journey and emerged on the other side of it.

You make the same journey every night. The question is whether you know it.

This is the claim at the center of *Hours*, and it is worth stating plainly: a day is a complete cosmological cycle. It has a shape. That shape is not arbitrary — it is the shape of death and return, of descent and emergence, of darkness giving way to light not because light overcomes darkness but because darkness produces it.

The practical consequences of this understanding are significant. If a day is a passage rather than a container, then how you cross the thresholds matters. The moment you enter the night is not simply the moment you stop being awake — it is a genuine crossing, a movement from the manifest world into something older and less visible. The moment you wake is not simply the resumption of activity — it is a return, a re-entry into the living hours carrying whatever the night has worked in you.

Most daily practice has no theology underneath it. Morning routines and evening rituals float free of any structural understanding of what a day actually demands. They may be useful. They may even be beautiful. But without the framework, they remain techniques rather than theology — things you do rather than ways you understand what you are inside of.

Hours is the framework.

The chapters that follow move through the cosmological structure of a day in sequence — through Egyptian, Greek, and Celtic traditions, through the specific theology of each threshold, through the work the night does and what it means to return from it. Each chapter builds on this one.

But this one contains the whole of it. A day is a passage. You are already inside one. The only question is whether you cross it awake.

The Night Has Geography

The night is not what remains when the day ends. It is where the day is made.

The night is not empty.

This seems obvious until you examine what most people actually believe about sleep. Strip away the language of rest and recovery — the modern, physiological account — and what remains is a picture of absence. You lose consciousness. Hours pass. You return. What happened in between is, for most practical purposes, nothing.

The Egyptians knew better. Not as a matter of faith but as a matter of cartography. The night has geography. It has twelve hours, each distinct, each inhabited, each requiring something specific from the one who passes through it. The solar barque of Ra does not drift through darkness. It navigates.

The Duat — the Egyptian underworld, the deep structure beneath the visible world — is not a place of punishment or waiting. It is the mechanism of renewal. It is where the sun goes to be remade. Without the Duat, there is no dawn. The passage through darkness is not incidental to the sun's existence. It is what makes the sun possible.

Each of the twelve hours of the night has a name, a guardian, and a gate. Ra's barque must be recognized, challenged, and admitted at each threshold. The gods who crew the barque have specific roles. The spells that protect the passage are precise and non-negotiable. This is not mythology in the sense of symbolic narrative. It is theology in the sense of structural description — an account of how reality actually works at the level that matters most.

Hour by hour, Ra moves deeper into the Duat. In the fifth hour he reaches the tomb of Osiris — the still center, the place of deepest rest, where even the sun must stop and be reconstituted before it can continue. This is not death in the sense of ending. It is death in the sense of transformation — the dissolution that makes renewal possible. You cannot emerge from the night unchanged. The Duat does not permit it.

By the twelfth hour, Ra has passed through the body of the serpent Apophis — the force of chaos and dissolution that threatens the passage every single night — and emerges from its mouth as Khepri, the scarab, the god of the rising sun. Not the same god who entered. Not Ra-who-set but Ra-who-rises, reborn from the passage itself.

This is the Egyptian account of every morning you have ever woken to.

What does it mean for how you understand your own nights? Not that you are Ra, and not that you must believe in the literal geography of the Duat. What it means is this: the tradition that looked most carefully at the structure of the night concluded that it has structure. That what happens in darkness follows a pattern. That there are depths in the night that correspond to genuine depths in experience — places where something in you must stop, be reconstituted, pass through its own version of the fifth hour before it can continue toward dawn.

The Duat is a map. You do not need to memorize it to benefit from knowing it exists. What matters is the underlying claim: the night is not empty passage. It is not a gap between days. It is the place where the day is made.

Greek tradition arrived at a parallel understanding through different means. Where the Egyptians gave the night a geography, the Greeks gave it inhabitants. Nyx — Night herself, one of the first beings to emerge from Chaos — is not a void. She is a presence, a power, a mother. Her children populate the night with everything the living hours cannot contain: sleep and death, dream and fate, strife and retribution. The night is not where these forces go when they are not needed. It is where they live. It is their home.

We will spend more time with Nyx in the next chapter. But her existence here is important as a corroboration of the Egyptian insight. Two traditions, looking at the same darkness, arriving at the same conclusion: there is something there. The night is inhabited. It has its own order, its own residents, its own work to do.

You cross it every night. The barque moves whether you are paying attention or not. The gates open and close on their own schedule. What changes when you understand this is not the passage itself but your relationship to it — the difference between being carried through a place you do not know and traveling through a place you have been given a name for.

The night has geography. You are somewhere in it right now, or you will be tonight, or you were last night. The passage is already underway.

The question, as always, is whether you cross it awake.

The night is not what remains when the day ends. It is where the day is made.

The Night Has Inhabitants

The night is inhabited. It has its own order, its own residents, its own work to do.

Before the gods there was Chaos. And from Chaos came Nyx.

Night is not a late arrival in Greek cosmology. She is among the first things. In Hesiod's account she emerges directly from the primordial void — not created, not ruled over, not subordinate to anything that came before her. She is original. She is, in the Greek understanding of reality, one of the conditions of existence rather than one of its contents.

Even Zeus is careful around Nyx. There is a moment in the *Iliad* where Hypnos — Sleep, one of Nyx's sons — takes refuge with his mother after angering the king of the gods, and Zeus does not pursue him. Not because he cannot. Because Nyx is older than his authority, and he knows it. The night precedes the Olympian order. It will outlast it.

This is the first thing to understand about the Greek contribution to the theology of the night: darkness is not the absence of divine presence. It is one of the oldest divine presences there is.

Nyx's children are worth knowing by name, because each one is a distinct force that inhabits your nights whether you have named it or not.

Hypnos is Sleep — not the act of sleeping but the god of it, the power that draws you under. His twin is Thanatos, Death. They are not opposites in the Greek understanding. They are siblings, nearly identical in form, different only in whether the crossing they facilitate is temporary or permanent. Every night you pass through Hypnos into something that resembles his brother closely enough that the Greeks saw them as family. The observation is precise. Sleep is a small death. You have always known this. The Greeks simply named it.

Morpheus is one of the Oneiroi — the gods of dreams — and his name is the root of our word for form. He is a shaper of appearances, capable of taking any human likeness in the dream state. When the gods want to send a message through sleep they send Morpheus. Dreams, in this framework, are not the random firing of a resting brain. They are communications from a populated darkness, delivered by a specific messenger to a specific recipient for a specific purpose.

The Moirai — the Fates — are also children of Nyx in some traditions. Clotho, who spins the thread of life. Lachesis, who measures it. Atropos, who cuts it. If the Fates are daughters of Night, then the deepest determinations of a human life are worked out in darkness, away from the visible world, in the hours when you are not watching.

Nemesis, too. And Eris, strife. And the Keres, spirits of violent death. Nyx's household is not comfortable. It contains forces that the daylight world would prefer to ignore — fate, death, strife, the violent end of things. The night does not exclude these. It is where they live. It is their proper home.

What does it mean that you enter this household every night?

It means, first, that the darkness you cross is not empty but populated — that the forces you meet in dream and in the depths of sleep have names and natures, that they are doing their own work regardless of whether you are aware of them. Hypnos is putting you under whether you have thanked him or not. The Oneiroi are moving through the dream space whether you remember what they showed you or not. The Moirai are at their work in the deep hours regardless of your relationship to the concept of fate.

It means, second, that there is a reason the night feels different from the day. The daylight world is the world of the Olympians — ordered, hierarchical, governed by the bright logic of Zeus. The night is older than that order. When you cross into it you cross into something that predates the structures you navigate during the living hours. This is not a regression. It is an access. The night gives you contact with forces that the day cannot contain.

It means, third, that how you enter the night matters. Not because the inhabitants of Nyx's household will treat you differently based on your attitude — they will do their work regardless — but because your awareness of where you are changes your capacity to bring something back from it. The person who falls into sleep as into a void and wakes without reflection is still being worked on by the same forces. They simply have no framework for what was done to them, no way to integrate it, no relationship to the passage they just completed.

Nyx does not require your belief. Her household runs on its own schedule. But she rewards attention.

This has been the consistent teaching across every tradition *Hours* draws on: the night is real, it is structured, it is inhabited, and the crossing of it is consequential. The Egyptians mapped it. The Greeks named its residents. The Celts built their entire sacred calendar around the principle that it is where everything begins.

You enter it tonight. You entered it last night. You will enter it again and again for as long as you are alive.

The question is not whether you cross it. The question is whether you cross it as someone who knows where they are.

IV

The Threshold at Dusk

The threshold is where transformation happens.

There is a moment in the evening when the light changes.

Not the moment the sun sets — that is a celestial event, measurable and precise. This is something subtler: the moment when the quality of the air shifts, when the world seems briefly to hold its breath, when the colors of things become more vivid even as they begin to fade. Anyone who has paid attention has felt it. Most people do not have a name for it.

The Celts had a name for it. They had a theology for it. And they built their entire understanding of time around it.

The Celtic day begins at sundown. Not at midnight, not at sunrise, but at the moment the sun drops below the horizon and the threshold between the living world and the deeper world becomes permeable. This is not an arbitrary calendrical choice. It is a theological statement about the nature of reality: darkness is origin, not conclusion. The day does not end at dusk. It begins there.

Every sabbat on the Wheel of the Year starts at sundown for the same reason. Samhain begins not on the morning of October 31st but on the evening of it — at the threshold, at the moment when the veil is thinnest, at the point of maximum permeability between the world you can see and the world that underlies it. The sacred moment is always the threshold. The threshold is always at dusk.

What is a threshold, exactly?

It is not a line. A line divides two spaces cleanly — you are on one side or the other, and the transition between them is instantaneous. A threshold is different. A threshold is a place where two realities are simultaneously present, where neither fully governs, where the rules of both apply and neither completely. The word comes from the practice of threshing grain — the threshold was literally the place where the work of separation happened, where what was useful was distinguished from what was not. It is a place of transformation, not merely of passage.

Dusk is a threshold in this sense. It is not the moment day ends and night begins. It is the brief span — sometimes minutes, sometimes longer — when both are present. The light is still there but weakening. The darkness is arriving but has not yet taken hold. You are between states. The world is between states. This is, in Celtic understanding, when the most important things become possible.

The practical consequence of this theology is significant. If dusk is a threshold rather than a transition, then how you cross it matters. The person who moves from afternoon into evening without awareness — closing a laptop, turning on lights, beginning the domestic sequence of dinner and television and eventual sleep — is crossing the threshold without knowing it. The passage still happens. The night still begins. But the opportunity of the threshold is missed.

What does it mean to cross the threshold at dusk with awareness?

It means, first, acknowledging that something is ending. The living hours have a shape, and dusk marks their completion. Whatever the day held — its work, its encounters, its demands — is now closing. Not forever, not irrevocably, but for now. The sun has done what it came to do. You can release it.

It means, second, acknowledging that something is beginning. Not merely the absence of day but the presence of night — with its own structure, its own inhabitants, its own work. You are not retreating from the world at dusk. You are entering a different layer of it. The Duat is opening. Nyx's household is stirring. The barque is preparing to depart.

It means, third, standing still for a moment at the threshold itself. Not rushing through it in either direction. The liminal is not comfortable — it is, by definition, the place where the usual categories do not apply, where you are neither here nor there. But it is precisely this discomfort that makes it generative. The threshold is where transformation happens. You cannot be transformed if you never stop moving long enough to be changed.

The Celts did not experience dusk as the end of the day. They experienced it as the beginning of everything. The sacred calendar, the festival cycle, the whole architecture of their relationship to time was built on this understanding. Darkness is where the year turns. Darkness is where the season shifts. Darkness is where the gods are closest and the veil is thinnest.

Darkness is where the day is made.

You stand at this threshold every evening. The light changes. The air shifts. The world holds its breath for a moment between what it was and what it is becoming.

The question is whether you stop long enough to notice.

V

The Work of the Night

Sleep is not a pause in your life. It is where a significant portion of your life's work is done.

While you sleep, something is working.

The body does its most significant repair work in the deep hours — cellular regeneration, memory consolidation, the processing of the day's experience into something the waking mind can integrate. Science has confirmed what the traditions always knew: sleep is not the absence of activity. It is a different kind of activity, one that the waking state cannot accomplish and does not have access to.

But the traditions were not talking about cellular regeneration. They were talking about something that happens at a level the body's biology only partially describes.

In Egyptian cosmological thinking, the hours you spend in sleep correspond to the hours Ra spends in the Duat. You are not merely resting while the sun completes its rotation. You are, in some sense that the tradition took seriously, participating in the same passage. The Duat is not only the sun's underworld. It is the underworld — the deep structure beneath all visible existence — and every being that crosses from the living world into sleep crosses into its territory.

What happens there?

The fifth hour of the Duat is the hour of the tomb of Osiris. This is the still center, the deepest rest, the moment of maximum dissolution before the process of reconstitution begins. In the Egyptian understanding, this corresponds to the deepest stage of sleep — the place where you are most fully released from the structures of waking identity, most fully available to be remade.

Osiris is the god of the dead, but more precisely he is the god of resurrection — the deity who was killed, dismembered, reassembled, and restored to a new kind of life. His tomb is not a place of ending. It is the workshop of renewal. To pass through the tomb of Osiris is to be taken apart and put back together in a form that can survive the remainder of the passage and emerge at dawn.

You do not remember this happening. You are not meant to. The work of the deep night is not available to the conscious mind because the conscious mind is precisely what must be suspended for the work to proceed. You cannot be disassembled while you are watching. The ego that monitors and manages and narrates your waking experience must release its grip entirely before the deeper work can begin.

This is why the Celts understood sleep as a genuine death — not the permanent death of Thanatos but the temporary death of Hypnos, the nightly dissolution that makes continued existence possible. You do not wake as the same person who slept. The night has worked on you. Something has been released that was no longer useful. Something has been reinforced that needed strengthening. The proportions of what you are have shifted, almost imperceptibly, in the direction of what you are becoming.

The Greeks located this work in the Oneiroi — the dream gods, children of Nyx — whose job is not entertainment but instruction. Morpheus takes the form of people you know to deliver messages you need to receive. Phobetor sends dreams that frighten because fear is sometimes the only way to make a person pay attention. Phantasos sends dreams of the inanimate world — landscapes, objects, the textures of things — because sometimes what needs to be communicated cannot be communicated through human form.

Dreams, in this framework, are not random. They are the night's primary mode of communication with the waking mind. They are the record of work being done — imperfectly translated into images and narratives that the conscious mind can partially access upon waking. The translation is always lossy. What you remember of a dream is a small fraction of what the dream contained. But even the fragment can be instructive if you approach it as instruction rather than noise.

What does all of this mean practically?

It means that the quality of your entry into the night affects the quality of the work the night can do. This is not about sleep hygiene in the modern sense. It is about the state in which you present yourself at the threshold. A person who enters the night carrying unprocessed anger, unacknowledged grief, the unresolved tension of the day's encounters — that person is presenting the night's workers with a more complicated task. The work will still be done. But more of the night's resources will be spent on what could have been addressed at the threshold.

The dusk practice — standing at the threshold, releasing the day, acknowledging what is beginning — is not preparatory in the sense of getting ready for rest. It is preparatory in the sense of presenting yourself clearly for the work. You are entering a workshop. The workers there are skilled and the work they do is real. Arriving with awareness of what you carry into the night is a form of respect for the process.

It also means that the quality of your emergence from the night matters. The work done in sleep does not automatically integrate into waking consciousness. It is available — carried back across the threshold with you — but it requires attention to access. The moment of waking is a moment of return, and what you do with the first minutes of that return determines how much of the night's work you will be able to use.

We will spend more time with that threshold in the next chapter. For now, the point is simply this: the night is a workshop. You are both the worker and the material. The traditions that looked carefully at this understood it as the most consequential part of the day — the part that makes the rest possible.

Sleep is not a pause in your life. It is where a significant portion of your life's work is done.

*Awareness does not change the passage. It
changes what you carry through it.*

The Threshold at Dawn

Stand here for a moment before you cross it. The living hours will wait.

You have been somewhere.

This is the first thing to understand about waking. Not that consciousness is resuming after a gap, not that the body has rested and is ready to function again, but that you are returning from a passage — crossing back across a threshold that you crossed in the other direction at dusk, carrying whatever the night worked into you.

Ra emerges from the mouth of Apophis as Khepri. Not Ra-who-set. Not the same deity who entered the Duat twelve hours before. The passage has changed him. He is the scarab now — the god of the rising sun, of becoming, of the thing that is in the process of being made. Khepri's name means something like *he who is coming into being*. Dawn is not a return to what was. It is the arrival of something new, made possible by what the night dissolved and reconstituted in the dark.

This is what you are at the moment of waking. Not restored to yesterday's self. Not refreshed and ready to resume. You are Khepri — in the process of becoming, carrying the work of the night into the light of the living hours, not yet fully formed into what this day will make you.

The threshold at dawn is as real as the threshold at dusk, and it asks as much of you.

In Celtic understanding, dawn is the completion of what dusk began. The day that started at sundown is now arriving at its most visible expression. The long work of the night — the passage through the dark, the dissolution and reconstitution, the movement through Nyx's household — has produced this moment. The light is not the opposite of the darkness that preceded it. It is what the darkness made.

This changes how the first moments of waking should be understood.

Most people treat waking as the start of the day's productivity — the moment when the useful hours begin and the lost hours of sleep are finally over. The alarm sounds and the mind immediately reaches forward: what needs to be done, what was left unfinished yesterday, what the day will demand. The threshold is crossed at speed, without looking back, without acknowledgment of where you have just been.

But you have just been somewhere. The night has done its work. You are carrying something back across the threshold — something that the dream state translated imperfectly into images, something that the deep work of the Duat has shifted in your cellular memory, something that Morpheus delivered that you may or may not remember but that is present in you nonetheless.

The threshold at dawn is the moment when that material is most accessible. Before the demands of the day assert themselves, before the waking mind reassembles its usual structures and priorities, there is a brief window — sometimes only minutes — when what the night worked in you is close to the surface. The Egyptians understood this. The *Amduat*, the text that describes Ra's journey through the Duat, ends not with the sunrise but with the moment just before it — the moment of maximum potential, when the passage is complete but the day has not yet begun.

What do you do at the threshold at dawn?

The first thing is to not immediately leave it. The instinct is to cross it as quickly as possible — to reach for the phone, to begin the mental accounting of the day ahead, to move from horizontal to vertical as efficiently as possible. This instinct is understandable and almost always wrong. The threshold is where transformation is available. Leaving it immediately closes the window before you have looked through it.

The second thing is to notice what you are carrying. Not to analyze it, not to journal it extensively, not to perform a lengthy ritual of integration. Simply to notice. What is the texture of this morning? What is present that was not present last night, or present differently? What did the night leave you with? A fragment of dream, a shifted feeling, a sense of resolution or of something newly opened — whatever it is, it is the night's communication, and the threshold at dawn is when it is most legible.

The third thing is to acknowledge the crossing. You have returned. The passage is complete for this cycle. Ra has emerged as Khepri. The Celtic day that began at last night's dusk has arrived at its most visible moment. Something was dissolved in the dark and has come back through the threshold changed. This deserves a moment of recognition — not ceremony necessarily, not ritual in the formal sense, but the simple acknowledgment that something real happened while you slept and that you are not exactly the person who fell asleep last night.

There is a posture that belongs to this threshold. Place one hand at the chest, or both, one over the other. Take one full breath. This is not a technique. It is the recognition that breath is the body's first declaration of presence — the act by which a newborn signals that it has arrived in the visible world, and the act by which you, every morning, do the same. You have crossed the night. The body is taking its first conscious breath of the new cycle. That breath is the same breath an infant takes. It is the gesture of having arrived.

The chest is where this posture lands because the chest is where the breath rises and falls visibly, where the heartbeat is most audible to the body's own attention, where the practitioner most directly feels themselves coming back into waking life. Other moments in the practice will move through other places in the body. This one stays at the chest. The threshold at dawn is the threshold of return, and return begins with breath.

You are Khepri. You are coming into being. The day that follows is the expression of the night that preceded it, and the night that preceded it was working toward exactly this moment.

The threshold at dawn is not the beginning of the useful hours. It is the culmination of the entire passage — the point toward which the whole cycle has been moving since the light changed at dusk and you stood at the threshold of the night.

Stand here for a moment before you cross it.

The living hours will wait.

The Living Hours

Full presence in the living hours is not a productivity practice. It is a theological act.

The sun is up. The world is visible. You are here.

This is not nothing. After the long passage through the night, after the dissolution and reconstitution, after the crossing of the threshold at dawn — arrival in the living hours is an achievement. You have completed the most consequential part of the day's cycle before most people have thought to call it a day at all.

The Greeks gave the sun a driver. Helios — not Apollo, who is a god of many things of which the sun is only one, but Helios, whose sole function is the daily crossing — takes his chariot from the eastern threshold each morning and drives it in a great arc across the sky to the western horizon. The journey takes the full span of the living hours. It is a description of what the living hours actually are: a crossing, a passage through the visible world, a traversal that mirrors and completes the invisible crossing of the night.

In some versions of the myth, Helios at the end of his day's journey does not simply stop. He boards a great cup — the Cup of Oceanus — and rides the stream of the world-ocean back around the earth to the east, ready to begin again. The living hours are bounded on both sides by water, by the great circular current that underlies the visible world. The day is not a line from dawn to dusk. It is a segment of a circle, and the circle never stops moving.

This is what it means to be fully present in the living hours: to understand that you are on the arc, not at the center of it.

The modern error about the living hours is not that they are undervalued — if anything, the modern world overvalues them, treating them as the only hours that count and the rest as necessary interruption. The error is more specific: the living hours are treated as the place where the real work happens, and everything else — the night, the thresholds, the passage — is understood as preparation for or recovery from them.

This has it backwards.

The living hours are the expression of the night's work, not its purpose. What you bring to the manifest world in the span between dawn and dusk was shaped in the dark. The clarity or confusion of your thinking, the openness or contraction of your capacity for encounter, the energy available for what the day asks — all of it was worked on while you slept, processed through the night's machinery, and delivered back to you at the threshold of dawn. The living hours are the harvest of the night, not the other way around.

This does not diminish them. If anything it elevates them — but differently than the modern account does. The modern account says the living hours matter because they are where things get done. The theological account says the living hours matter because they are where the invisible work of the night becomes visible — where what was dissolved and reconstituted in the dark takes form in the world.

Full presence in the living hours, understood this way, is not a productivity practice. It is a theological act. You are the sun at its height, carrying the work of the night into its fullest expression. The encounters of the day, the work you do, the relationships you inhabit — these are the visible face of a cycle that has been turning since last night's dusk. To be absent from them, distracted, half-present, moving through the living hours without awareness — this is not just a personal failing. It is a failure to complete the passage.

Helios does not stop halfway across the sky. He drives the full arc. The living hours demand their full traversal.

What does full presence in the living hours actually mean?

It means carrying the threshold at dawn with you into the day — not dwelling on it, not making the living hours into an extension of the morning's liminal state, but remaining aware that you emerged from somewhere and that the quality of that emergence is present in everything you bring to the day.

It means understanding the living hours as finite — bounded by dusk, which is already coming, which will arrive whether or not you have finished what you wanted to do. The arc has an end. Helios will reach the western horizon. The threshold at dusk will open again. The day is not a container you can fill indefinitely. It is a passage with a shape, and the shape includes its ending.

It means treating midday — the sun at its height, Helios at the apex of the arc — as a threshold of its own, a moment of maximum presence, maximum visibility, maximum expression of what the cycle has produced. Not a time to push harder but a time to notice where you are. You are at the top of the arc. The night is equidistant in both directions. This moment, precisely this one, is what the entire passage has been moving toward.

The living hours are the gift of the night's work made visible. They are brief. They are real. They are bounded on both sides by thresholds that ask something of you.

*Morning is not where a day starts. It is what
a day has been working toward all night.*

The Practice of the Passage

Awareness does not change the passage. It changes what you carry through it.

You have the framework now.

Eight chapters have established what a day actually is — not a container of time but a cosmological passage, not a neutral span but a structured cycle with a shape, a theology, and specific demands. The night has geography. It has inhabitants. It has work to do. The thresholds of dusk and dawn are real crossings, not transitions. The living hours are the visible expression of what the dark produced. The deep hours of the Midnight Passage are where what could not continue is dissolved and what will continue is being remade. The circle never stops turning.

What do you do with this?

The answer is not a routine. It is not a list of practices to perform in sequence, a morning ritual checklist or an evening wind-down protocol. The traditions that gave us this framework did not produce self-help. They produced theology — which is to say, an account of the structure of reality that, when genuinely understood, changes how you move through the world without requiring you to follow instructions.

The practice that follows from *Hours* is not something you add to your day. It is a way of understanding the day you are already living.

There are four points on the cycle that ask for attention. Not ceremony, not elaborate ritual — attention. A quality of awareness brought to four specific moments in the daily passage where the structure of what is happening is most legible, most available, most capable of being met rather than merely undergone. Three of them you meet awake. The fourth you meet at its threshold and consent to enter.

The first is dusk.

The light changes. The air shifts. The world holds its breath between what it was and what it is becoming. This is the threshold the Celts understood as the beginning of everything — the moment when darkness asserts itself as origin, not conclusion. What the threshold at dusk asks of you is release. The living hours are closing. Whatever they held — their demands, their disappointments, their unfinished business — is now moving into the past. The night that is opening has its own work to do, and it does that work more cleanly when you arrive at the threshold having acknowledged what you are leaving behind.

This does not require much time. It requires presence. A moment of genuine acknowledgment that something is ending and something is beginning — that you are crossing from the visible world into the older world, from the Olympian order into the territory of Nyx, from the arc of Helios into the barque of Ra. The threshold is real. Standing at it consciously is the practice.

The second is the Midnight Passage.

This is the one you almost never cross consciously, and that is not a failure of the practice. It is the nature of the crossing. Midnight is the fifth hour of the Duat, the tomb of Osiris, the still center where dissolution is most complete and reconstitution begins. The work that happens here cannot be witnessed by the waking mind. It happens to you while the structures that ordinarily monitor experience are suspended. That suspension is not incidental. It is required.

What the Midnight Passage asks is not attention in the same sense the other three moments ask for it. It asks for two smaller things. The first is a brief, conscious entry into the crossing at the threshold before sleep — an offering, the consent to be worked on, the recognition that you are descending into a workshop older than you. The second is a particular quality of recognition if you find yourself awake within the deep hours, when the practice surfaces you briefly into Nyx's household before letting you return. The night is doing its work whether you sleep through the remainder or witness a portion of it. The acknowledgment is what the practice asks. Not vigilance. Not effort. Recognition.

The Midnight Passage is the deepest movement of the cycle and the one most often missed precisely because it does not require your conscious participation to be real. It is the work the other three moments are organized around — the dissolution dusk releases you toward, the reconstitution dawn receives you from, the apex midday expresses what was made there. You do not have to do anything for it to happen. The practice is only this: knowing it is happening, and meeting it at the threshold before you descend.

The third is dawn.

You have returned. The passage is complete. Ra has emerged as Khepri — not the same god who entered, but the god the passage made. You are, at the moment of waking, in the same condition: carrying the night's work back across the threshold into the living hours, not yet fully formed into what this day will make you. The threshold at dawn asks for the same quality of attention as the threshold at dusk, but in the opposite direction. Not release but reception. What did the night leave you with? What is present this morning that was not present last night, or present differently? The window is brief. Before the day's demands reassemble themselves and claim your attention entirely, there is a moment when the night's communication is close to the surface and legible. Meet it there.

The fourth is midday.

This one is easy to miss because it does not feel like a threshold. There is no light changing, no crossing from one state to another. But midday is the apex of the arc — the sun at its height, Helios at the furthest point from both thresholds, the moment of maximum presence in the manifest world. What midday asks is not release or reception but simply this: notice where you are. You are on the arc. The night is equidistant in both directions. Everything the passage produced — every night that worked on you, every threshold you crossed, every morning you returned from the dark — is present in you right now, at midday, expressed in how you are moving through the living hours. This moment is what the whole cycle has been producing. Be here for it.

Four points. Three brief returns to awareness of the passage you are always already inside, and one offering at the threshold of the deepest crossing. No elaborate preparation required, no special conditions, no lengthy ritual. The practice is simply this: know what you are crossing when you cross it. Meet the dissolution at its threshold and consent to it. Receive what it produces. Stand at the apex and be on the arc.

This is what *Hours* has been building toward — not a new set of things to do but a new way of understanding what is already happening. The passage does not require your participation to proceed. Ra travels through the Duat whether anyone is watching or not. Nyx's household does its work regardless of whether you have acknowledged it. The Celtic day begins at sundown on a schedule that has nothing to do with your awareness of it.

But you are not Ra. You are a human being moving through a cosmological structure that is larger than you and indifferent to your understanding of it. The difference your understanding makes is not to the structure — it is to you. The person who crosses the threshold at dusk knowing what they are crossing arrives at the night's work in a different condition than the person who stumbles into sleep without acknowledgment. The person who consents to the Midnight Passage at its threshold descends differently than the person who does not. The person who stands at the threshold at dawn knowing they have returned from somewhere receives the night's communication in a way that the person already reaching for their phone does not.

Awareness does not change the passage. It changes what you carry through it.

The day is already underway. The threshold at dusk is coming, or it has just passed, or you are standing at it right now. The barque is preparing to depart. Nyx's household is stirring. The work of the night is waiting.

You know what you are inside of now.

Cross it awake.

PART II

The Egyptian Frame

The Two Vessels

You do not cross the night in the same form you crossed the day.

Ra has two barques. This is not a detail of Egyptian mythology. It is a structural claim about what the passage requires.

The Mandjet — the Barque of Millions of Years — carries Ra from the eastern horizon to the western. It is the vessel of the living hours. It moves through visible sky, through light, through the territory where things can be seen and named and acted upon. It is the vehicle suited to the day.

At the western horizon, Ra leaves it.

He does not repair the Mandjet for the night journey. He does not modify it. He boards a different vessel — the Mesektet, the Night Barque — because the territory he is about to enter cannot be navigated in the form that served him during the day.

This is the first thing the barque tradition teaches: the night is not a continuation of the day by other means. It is a different territory requiring a different vessel. What carried you through the living hours — your competence, your alertness, your capacity to manage and decide and act — is not what will carry you through the dark. The faculties suited to daylight do not function in the Duat.

A different set is required, and they are already on board. They have always been on board. But they do not serve the Mandjet. They serve only the passage.

Consider what this means practically. Every evening, whether you mark it or not, you leave one vessel and board another. The transition happens at dusk — the threshold you already know from the Hours theology. What the barque tradition adds is the claim that this is not merely a shift in attention or mood. It is a change of vehicle. The thing that moves you through the night is structurally different from the thing that moved you through the day.

The Mandjet is powered by Ra's visible presence — the sun in the sky, the force of light acting on the world. The Mesektet is powered by something else entirely. It moves through dark water, through regions where light does not reach, through territories governed by presences who do not answer to the solar order. It requires a crew whose skills are specific to this territory: perception that works without sight, utterance that functions in silence, magic that operates in dissolution rather than construction.

You have experienced this difference. You have lain down at night still running the day's machinery — planning, calculating, reviewing, managing — and felt the machinery fail. Not because you are tired, though you may be tired. Because the machinery is built for the Mandjet. It does not function on the Mesektet. The passage does not require your management. It requires your presence in a different mode: receptive, consenting, stripped of the instruments that serve you in the light.

This is not a failure of the day-self. It is a change of vessel. The Mandjet served you well. It will serve you again tomorrow. But it cannot go where you are going to-night.

The barque tradition also teaches that the change happens at a specific threshold — the western horizon, the place where the sun enters the earth. In the *Amduat*, this moment is depicted with precision: the sun descends, the western mountain opens, the Mesektet is waiting. The crew is already assembled. The passage does not wait for you to be ready. The vessel is there whether you board it consciously or are carried aboard by sleep.

The difference is in what you carry through.

A practitioner who marks the dusk threshold — who recognizes the vessel change as it happens — crosses into the night with awareness of what has shifted. The faculties of the day are set down. The faculties of the night are acknowledged. This is not a ritual addition to the existing Dusk Rite. It is a deepening of what the

Dusk Rite already does: you are not merely releasing the day. You are leaving one vessel and boarding another.

At dawn, the reverse. The Mesektet has carried you through the twelve hours of the Duat. The eastern horizon opens. Ra boards the Mandjet again — reconstituted, carrying what the night made. The vessel suited to the living hours receives him in his renewed form. What was worked in the dark is now available to the light.

You have experienced this too. The morning when something has shifted overnight — a clarity that was not available yesterday, a weight that has been set down without your conscious effort, a knowing that arrived while you slept. This is what the Mesektet carried. This is what the night crew worked. The Mandjet receives it and takes it into the day.

Two vessels. One for the territory of light, one for the territory of the dark. The same god in both, but not the same form. Not the same crew. Not the same power source. Not the same navigation.

The passage requires both.

The Crew of the Mesektet

Ra does not cross the night alone. Neither do you.

The Mesektet carries a company. This is not ornamental — it is structural. The night barque requires specific faculties to navigate the Duat, and those faculties are not Ra's own. They belong to distinct intelligences who serve the passage, each with a function that cannot be performed by another.

This is worth sitting with before you meet them individually. The solar theology of the living hours can look, from the outside, like a theology of singular power — one god, one arc, one blazing presence crossing the sky. And during the day, carried on the Mandjet, that impression holds. Ra's visible light is the dominant fact of the living hours. Everything else orients around it.

But the night undoes that arrangement. In the Duat, Ra is not the blazing sovereign. He is the passenger. He travels in a diminished form — often depicted as ram-headed, aged, or enclosed within the coils of the protective serpent Mehen. His light does not illuminate the regions he passes through. His authority does not command the inhabitants of the territories he crosses. He is undergoing the passage, not directing it.

What directs it is the crew.

Sia stands at the prow. Sia is divine perception — not sight, which requires light, but the deeper faculty of knowing what is there. In the Duat, where light fails, Sia is what remains. He perceives the territory ahead: its dangers, its inhabitants, its requirements. He knows what is coming before it arrives.

The practitioner's equivalent of Sia is the faculty that operates in the dark when the conscious mind has gone quiet. It is what recognizes a dream as significant before the waking mind has interpreted it. It is the knowing that arrives at three in the morning — not analytical, not narrative, but direct. Sia does not explain what he perceives. He perceives it. The explanation, if it comes, belongs to the living hours.

If you have ever woken knowing something you did not know when you fell asleep — not a thought but a recognition, a shift in the ground of what you understood — you have experienced Sia's function. He was at the prow. He saw what was ahead. What he perceived became available to you at dawn, carried across on the Mandjet into the territory where you could finally use it.

Hu is authoritative utterance. Where Sia perceives, Hu speaks — and what Hu speaks becomes operative. This is not prayer, not petition, not the language of request. It is the creative word: the utterance that enacts. In Egyptian theology, Hu's speech does not describe reality. It constitutes it.

In the Duat, Hu's function is to name what is encountered. When the barque enters a new hour, Hu speaks the names of its inhabitants, its gates, its dangers. The naming is not informational — it is the act that allows safe passage. What is named correctly can be navigated. What is unnamed remains a threat.

The practitioner's equivalent of Hu is harder to locate because the modern relationship to language is almost entirely descriptive. We use words to report. Hu uses words to establish. The closest analogue in practice is the moment when you finally name something accurately — a grief, a pattern, a condition you have been living inside without language for it — and the naming itself changes your relationship to it. Not because understanding followed, but because the utterance was precise and the precision did its own work.

Hu does not speak often. When he does, it matters.

Heka is magic — but not in the colloquial sense. Heka is the connective force that binds intention to effect. He is older than the gods in some Egyptian accounts — a force that predates the divine order and makes the divine order possible. Without Heka, Sia's perception remains inert and Hu's utterance has no purchase. Heka is what makes the passage transformative rather than merely sequential.

In the Duat, Heka is what allows the work of the night to function: the dissolution that occurs at the fifth hour, the defense against Apophis at the seventh, the reconstitution that begins in the later hours. None of these are mechanical processes. They require a force that connects what is happening to what it means — that makes the passage through dark water an actual transformation rather than just a duration to be endured.

The practitioner's equivalent of Heka is the force that makes a practice real rather than performative. It is the difference between going through the motions of a rite and having the rite do something. You have felt this difference. Some nights the crossing is merely sleep. Other nights the crossing is operative — something is actually worked, actually dissolved, actually reconstituted. The difference is not in your effort or intention. It is in whether Heka is present.

You cannot summon Heka by trying harder. You can acknowledge that the force exists and that the passage depends on it. This acknowledgment is itself a form of consent.

Wepwawet is the Opener of the Ways. Jackal-headed, carried as a standard at the prow ahead of even Sia. His function is not perception but clearance — he opens the path that the barque will travel. In the Duat, where the passage is not guaranteed and the way forward can be blocked, sealed, or guarded, Wepwawet goes first.

The practitioner's equivalent of Wepwawet is whatever opens the way into sleep, into depth, into the territory where the night's work happens. For some practitioners this is a physical act — lying down, closing the eyes, releasing the body's hold on the vertical. For others it is the moment of genuine surrender that precedes sleep: the instant when the managing mind finally lets go and the way into the dark opens. Wepwawet does not force the way open. He opens what is ready to open. His function is not violence but readiness — being at the front of the passage so that when the way becomes available, it is taken.

The Steersman holds the tiller at the stern. In some *Amduat* recensions he is named; in others he is simply present — the one who keeps the barque on course through twelve hours of territory that has no landmarks visible to ordinary sight. He steers by knowledge of the passage itself, not by reference to anything external.

The practitioner's equivalent of the steersman is the faculty that keeps the night's work on course even when you are unconscious. You do not steer your dreams. You do not direct the dissolution that happens in deep sleep. Something does. The night's passage has a direction — from entry to the still center to reconstitution to dawn — and something holds that direction through all twelve hours. The steersman does not require your awareness to function. But acknowledging that the function exists — that the passage is steered, not random — changes the quality of trust you bring to the crossing.

These are the five primary faculties of the night barque. There are others — Hor-Hekenu, Horus in his praising aspect, sometimes at the helm; various protective deities who overlap with the defenders you will meet in the next chapter. But Sia, Hu, Heka, Wepwawet, and the steersman are the core crew. Between them they provide what the passage requires: perception in the dark, utterance that enacts, the connective force that makes transformation real, the opening of the way, and the holding of course.

Notice what is not on this list. Control is not on this list. Management is not on this list. Planning, executing, evaluating, optimizing — none of the faculties that serve the Mandjet are present on the Mesektet. The night does not require them. The night requires perception, speech, magic, pathfinding, and steady course. These are the intelligences that hold you while you sleep.

You do not need to invoke them by name to benefit from their work, any more than you need to name gravity to be held by it. They function whether or not you acknowledge them.

But acknowledgment changes the passage. A practitioner who knows the crew — who recognizes Sia's perception in a dream that carried knowing, who feels Heka's presence on a night when the crossing was real rather than merely restful, who senses the steersman holding course through a period of deep difficulty — inhabits the night differently than one who treats sleep as a blank.

The crew is already assembled. They have been assembled every night of your life. The Mesektet does not wait for you to learn their names. It waits for nothing. It sails.

What changes when you know who is on board is what you carry through.

The Defenders of the Passage

The passage is not safe. It was never meant to be.

The Mesektet does not carry only navigators. It carries defenders. This is not a precaution — it is a structural requirement of the journey. The Duat is contested territory. Something opposes the passage every night, and the opposition is real.

This is a claim most contemporary frameworks avoid. The night is treated as rest, as sanctuary, as the soft place where the day's noise quiets and healing occurs. And healing does occur — but it occurs inside a territory where something actively works against the completion of the passage. The barque is defended because it needs to be defended. Without the defense, the passage fails. Without the passage, there is no dawn.

Apophis is what opposes the passage.

He is not a demon in the later Christian sense — not a fallen being, not an agent of moral evil. He is the serpent of uncreation. His function is dissolution without reconstitution. Where Osiris dissolves what cannot continue so that what will continue can be remade, Apophis dissolves without purpose, without product, without return. He is entropy without architecture. He is the force that would unmake the passage itself — not redirect it, not corrupt it, but end it.

Every night, in the seventh hour of the Duat, Apophis attacks the barque.

This is worth letting land. Not occasionally. Not when conditions are unfavorable. Every night. The opposition to the passage is as reliable as the passage itself. The *Amduat* does not treat this as a crisis. It treats it as structure. The seventh hour is the hour of the great confrontation, and the confrontation happens on schedule, and the defense is mobilized on schedule, and the passage continues. The serpent is defeated. The serpent returns. The defeat is nightly. The return is nightly.

You have experienced this. You have had nights when the passage was opposed — when sleep would not come, or came and broke apart, or carried you into territory that felt hostile rather than restorative. Nights when something in you resisted the crossing, or something in the crossing resisted you. Nights that felt actively difficult in a way that "I didn't sleep well" does not capture. The barque tradition names what was happening: the passage was under attack. The force that opposes completion was doing what it does — and what it does is structural, not occasional. Every passage meets it. Every night.

The defenders exist because the attack exists.

Set stands at the prow of the Mesektet with a spear. This is the older Set — not the villain of the Osiris murder narrative, but the god whose function is violent defense of the solar order. In the Duat, Set's rage and strength, which make him dangerous in the living hours, become precisely what is needed. He is the only god strong enough to face Apophis directly. His spear pins the serpent. His voice drives it back. The very qualities that make Set a destabilizing force in the daylight world make him indispensable in the dark.

This is theologically significant. The faculty that defends the passage is contested. The Dusk Rite's soft consent and the receptive presence of the Pre-Sleep Acknowledgment do not apply here. It is ferocity in service of continuation. Set does not negotiate with Apophis. He does not understand Apophis. He drives his spear into the serpent's body and holds it there while the barque passes.

The practitioner's equivalent of Set is the force in you that refuses dissolution without purpose. Not the ego's resistance to change — that is something else, and the passage requires the ego to release. This is deeper: the part of you that knows the difference between transformative dissolution (Osiris's domain, the fifth-hour work) and purposeless unraveling (Apophis's domain, the seventh-hour attack). You have felt this distinction. There are nights when something needs to come apart, and the coming-apart is the work. There are other nights when something is trying to come apart that should not — when the unraveling is not productive but destructive, not a passage but a collapse. Set knows the difference. Set acts on the difference. Set does not hesitate.

Mehen is the protective serpent. Where Set faces Apophis head-on, Mehen's defense is enclosure. He coils around the cabin where Ra rests in his diminished form — the ram-headed, aged, vulnerable aspect that Ra assumes during the night journey. Mehen's body becomes the boundary that separates the god undergoing transformation from the forces that would interrupt it.

The practitioner's equivalent of Mehen is the protective structure around sleep itself. The dark room, the closed door, the body's withdrawal from the waking world, the biochemistry of melatonin and slow-wave sleep that creates a bounded space in which the night's work can proceed undisturbed. Mehen is not a faculty you exercise. He is a condition you maintain — or fail to maintain. A practitioner who sleeps with the phone beside the pillow, who leaves the door open to every interruption, who treats the sleeping space as continuous with the waking space, has compromised Mehen's coils. The cabin is unprotected. The god inside it is exposed.

This is not a prescription about sleep hygiene. It is a theological observation: the passage requires a bounded space in which transformation can occur without interruption. The *Amduat* depicts Mehen's coils with care because the protection is not optional. Ra cannot be reconstituted if the process is interrupted at the seventh hour. The defense must hold.

Isis and Nephthys flank the barque, often depicted at the prow and stern. Their function in the Duat is magical protection — not the physical defense of Set's spear or the bodily enclosure of Mehen's coils, but the sustained magical work that maintains the integrity of the passage. Isis speaks the words of power. Nephthys holds the mourning that keeps the dissolution sacred rather than chaotic. Together they maintain the ritual structure of the crossing — ensuring that what is happening in the Duat remains a passage rather than collapsing into mere destruction.

The practitioner's equivalent is harder to name precisely, because Isis and Nephthys are operating at a level most practitioners do not consciously access. Their work is closest to what happens when a night of genuine difficulty — grief, illness, crisis, the deep hours of a dark season — remains structurally intact rather than fragmenting into panic. Something holds the shape of the passage even when the content of the passage is terrible. Something ensures that the dissolution serves reconstitution. That something is doing magical work whether or not the practitioner recognizes it as such.

Notice the architecture of the defense. It is not a single function. It is four distinct operations working simultaneously:

Set's spear — direct confrontation with the force of uncreation.

Mehen's coils — physical enclosure of the vulnerable center.

Isis's words of power — magical maintenance of the passage's integrity.

Nephthys's mourning — holding the dissolution as sacred rather than chaotic.

These four are not redundant. Each addresses a different axis of threat. Apophis attacks the passage physically (Set defends), attacks the vulnerable god directly (Mehen defends), attacks the magical structure of the crossing (Isis defends), and attacks the meaning of the dissolution itself (Nephthys defends). The passage requires all four defenses because the opposition operates on all four levels.

This is the most uncomfortable claim of the barque tradition for most contemporary practitioners. The night is not only a place of work. It is a place of contest. Something opposes the passage, and the opposition is serious, and the defense engages with the seriousness the opposition requires. Every night. On schedule. Without fail on either side.

The comfort — if comfort is the right word — is that the defense is also on schedule. The defenders are already on the Mesektet. They boarded when you did. Set's spear is already in his hand. Mehen is already coiled. Isis is already speaking. Nephthys is already holding. The defense does not wait for your awareness any more than the attack does.

But a practitioner who knows the contest is happening inhabits the difficult night differently than one who believes the night should be peaceful and is bewildered when it is not. Some nights are the seventh hour. The serpent is real. The defense is also real. Both are structural. Both are every night.

The passage continues because the defense holds.

The Practitioner on the Barque

The crew serves the passage. The defenders protect the passage. You are the subject of the passage.

You have read three chapters now about the structure of the night barque. The vessel that changes at the western horizon. The crew whose faculties navigate the dark. The defenders whose work holds the passage against what would unmake it. Each of these has been described as if you were standing outside the image, watching the Mesektet move through the Duat as an observer reads a depiction in a tomb.

You are not outside the image.

This is the chapter that places you inside it. The previous three established the architecture of the passage; this one locates you within that architecture. The question the chapter asks is the question every practitioner eventually arrives at when the cosmological frame becomes specific enough to be inhabited: *where am I in this?* You have met the crew. You have met the defenders. You have read about the vessel and the dark water it crosses. But the *Amduat* depicts a vessel with figures aboard, and one of those figures is the god being carried, and the position you occupy is not the position you might assume.

The question the Hours theology asks is never whether the passage is happening. It is always what changes when you become conscious of it.

So: where are you on the barque?

You are not Sia. You are not Hu. You are not Heka or Wepwawet or the steersman. You are not Set with his spear or Mehen with his coils. These are intelligences with specific functions in the passage, and their functions are not yours. The crew does not need your help. The defenders do not need your assistance. The passage does not require your management, your direction, or your effort.

This is difficult for the practitioner who has been trained — by the culture, by other spiritual frameworks, by the deep habits of the managing mind — to believe that presence means participation, and participation means doing something. The Mesektet asks for a different kind of presence.

Ra himself models it. On the night barque, Ra is not commanding the crew. He is not steering. He is not fighting Apophis. He is enclosed within Mehen's coils, in his diminished form, undergoing the passage. His function during the twelve hours of the Duat is not authority but submission — not the submission of defeat, but the submission of a god who knows that what must happen to him can only happen if he allows it. He must be dissolved at the fifth hour. He must pass through the tomb of Osiris. He must be reconstituted in the later hours. None of this can occur if he is gripping the tiller.

The practitioner's position on the barque is analogous to Ra's, not to the crew's.

You are the one undergoing the passage. You are the one being carried. You are the one whose day-form must be released so that the night's work can proceed. The crew serves the passage. The defenders protect the passage. You are the subject of the passage — the one in whom the work is being done.

This reframes the practitioner's relationship to the night entirely. You are not performing the night's work. You are not directing it. You are not even witnessing it in any active sense, because for most of the passage you are unconscious. You are being worked on. The dissolution is happening to you. The reconstitution is happening to you. Sia perceives the territory on your behalf. Hu speaks the names that allow your safe passage. Heka makes the transformation real. Wepwawet opens the way you will travel. The steersman holds your course. Set drives back what would unmake you. Mehen encloses you while you are vulnerable. Isis maintains the integrity of the process. Nephthys holds the sacredness of your dissolution.

All of this happens while you sleep.

The practitioner's task — the only task — is to board the vessel consciously.

This is what the Dusk Rite does. This is what the Pre-Sleep Acknowledgment does. This is what the vessel change described in the first chapter of this orientation means in practice: you are not preparing for sleep. You are boarding the Mesektet. You are consenting to the passage. You are releasing the faculties of the Mandjet — the planning, the managing, the directing — and allowing the faculties of the night barque to take over.

And at dawn, you disembark. The Mesektet has carried you through twelve hours of territory you did not see, past dangers you did not fight, through a dissolution you did not direct and a reconstitution you did not engineer. You step onto the Mandjet carrying what the night made. The living hours begin. The crew and defenders of the Mesektet remain with the night vessel, ready for tonight.

There is a practice that belongs to this understanding, and it sits between the acknowledgment and devotional registers.

In the **acknowledgment register**, the practitioner recognizes the crew and defenders as presences whose work made the passage possible. This can be as simple as a moment at dawn — before the living hours claim you, before the Mandjet's faculties engage — in which you acknowledge that you were carried. That the night was navigated on your behalf. That perception, utterance, magic, pathfinding, and defense were operating while you slept. You do not need to name them. You need to recognize that the passage was not empty. It was staffed. It was held.

In the **devotional register**, the practitioner addresses the crew directly. This is not petitionary — you are not asking them to do their work, because their work does not depend on your asking. It is relational. It is the acknowledgment that these are intelligences, not mechanisms. Sia perceived the territory of your night. You can thank him for what he saw. Heka made the transformation real. You can honor the force that made it possible. Set drove back what would have unmade you. You can acknowledge the ferocity that held.

Both registers are real engagements. Neither is performance. The difference between them is the difference between recognizing a debt and addressing the one to whom it is owed. Both change the quality of the practitioner's relationship to the passage. Both make the crossing more conscious, which is the only thing the Hours theology has ever asked.

There is one more thing the barque tradition teaches about the practitioner's position, and it is perhaps the most important.

You board the Mesektet every night. But you also board it at other times — during illness, during grief, during the long passages of a life that require dissolution before reconstitution can begin. A divorce is a night journey. A collapse of vocation is a night journey. The death of someone you organized your world around is a night journey. These are passages through the Duat that last longer than a single night, and the barque carries you through them on the same terms: you are not directing the passage, the crew is working, the defenders are fighting, and your task is to consent to the crossing rather than grip the tiller of a vessel that no longer serves.

The twelve Hours of the Duat that follow this orientation are, on one level, a cosmological map of what happens between dusk and dawn each night. On another level, they are a map of any sustained passage through the dark — any period in which the living hours have dimmed and the territory you are crossing has no landmarks visible to ordinary sight. The barque carries you through both. The crew serves both. The defenders hold both.

You are already on the vessel.

The orientation is complete. The twelve hours begin.

The Hours of the Duat

The First Hour

> *The threshold is not the passage. It is the place where the passage begins.*

What the Amduat Describes

The first hour is the hour of entry. The Mesektet has crossed beneath the western horizon and now moves through the first region of the Duat — a long corridor that the *Amduat* calls *Wernes-of-the-Western-Mountain*, though some recensions name it differently. It is bounded territory: still close to the world the barque has just left, not yet in the deep regions where the night's work occurs.

The inhabitants of this hour are gods and goddesses of greeting. They line the corridor on either side of the river. They do not act on Ra. They welcome him. They announce his arrival to the further regions. They make the passage known.

This is the hour of arrival, not of work. The crew is at its stations. The defenders are in position. Apophis has not yet attacked — that confrontation belongs to the seventh hour. The dissolution at the tomb of Osiris is still four hours away. What happens in the first hour is the establishment of presence: Ra has entered the Duat, the territory has registered his arrival, the passage has begun.

The light here is described as muted but not absent. The sun has not yet been extinguished — Ra still carries his daylight form into this first region — but the visible light of the Mandjet is gone. What illuminates the first hour is the light Ra himself brings into the dark. It will not last. By the deeper hours it will be entirely consumed, and Ra will be carried in his most diminished form. But in the first hour, the transition has only just begun.

The Theological Claim

The first hour establishes the most easily missed claim of the entire Duat theology: **the passage has a beginning that is distinct from both the threshold and the deeper work.**

There is the dusk threshold — the moment of crossing, the change of vessel, the release of the day. The Hours foundation chapters and the Dusk Rite already address this.

There is the deeper night — the hours of dissolution, defense, and reconstitution, where the night's most consequential work occurs.

Between them is the first hour. And the first hour has its own theology.

What happens here is registration, not transformation. The territory acknowledges that you have entered. Something on the other side of the threshold notes your arrival. The passage that will work on you in the deeper hours first records that you are present.

This matters because contemporary frameworks tend to collapse this distinction. Sleep is treated as either the threshold (falling asleep) or the deep work (the meaningful hours of dreaming, dissolution, and recovery). The hour between — the long settling, the early sleep that is not yet deep, the territory where you have crossed but are not yet undergoing — is treated as latency. Filler. Time to be gotten through before the real work begins.

The Egyptian framework refuses this. The first hour is not preliminary to the passage. It is the passage in its first form: arrival, recognition, the establishment of presence in territory that until moments ago was not yours to inhabit.

The Barque in This Hour

The Mesektet moves slowly through Wernes. The crew is alert but not yet exercised — Sia perceives the welcoming gods, Hu speaks the names of greeting, Heka maintains the connective force, Wepwawet has opened the way and now travels at the prow. The steersman holds course. Set, Mehen, Isis, and Nephthys are at their stations but the threat has not yet arrived.

Ra himself sits in the cabin. He has not yet been enclosed in Mehen's coils — that protection becomes necessary later, when his form is at its most diminished. In the first hour, Ra is still recognizably himself, though the daylight crown has been set aside. The barque proceeds. The territory accepts its passage. The first hour begins.

Practitioner Application

The first hour of the Duat corresponds to the time after you have fallen asleep but before the deeper passage has begun — the early sleep that contemporary medicine calls non-REM stages one and two, the long settling, the territory where the body has released but the deepest work has not yet started.

You do not remember this hour, ordinarily. You did not direct it. You did not work in it. By the standards of conscious experience, nothing happened — you closed your eyes, time passed, eventually you arrived in the deeper hours where dreams and dissolution occur.

But something did happen. You were registered. The territory you crossed into acknowledged your arrival. The passage took note of you.

This is what the first hour offers the practitioner: the recognition that arrival itself is consequential. You do not need to do anything in the first hour. You do not need to direct anything. You do not need to be present in any active sense. The territory does its work whether you observe it or not. But knowing that the first hour exists — that there is a stage of the passage that is not threshold and not deep work but is the recognition of your presence in the dark — changes how you approach the early sleep.

The practitioner who has settled into bed and closed the eyes but has not yet been taken into deeper sleep is in the first hour. The work of this hour is not effort. It is consent to being seen by the territory you have just entered. Wernes acknowledges you. The welcoming gods register your passage. Something notes that you have come.

This is enough. Sleep continues from here. The deeper hours arrive in their own time.

In the **acknowledgment register**, the practitioner who wakes briefly during early sleep — or who notices the first hour as it is happening, in the long settling — can recognize: *I have been registered. The territory knows I have arrived.*

In the **devotional register**, the practitioner can offer: *The welcoming gods of the first hour, I have entered. Mark my passage.*

Neither requires elaboration. The first hour does not ask much.

A Guided Meditation for the First Hour

This meditation is for use as the practitioner settles into sleep, or as a deliberate practice on a night when the first hour is to be inhabited consciously. Read silently, recorded for personal use, or absorbed once and then carried into the dark.

Find a position you will not need to leave. Lie down if you are going to sleep. Sit comfortably if you are practicing while awake.

Let your weight settle. You do not need to relax in any particular way. You do not need to clear your mind. You only need to stop moving.

(pause)

Take three breaths. Do not control them. Let air arrive and leave in whatever rhythm your body is already using.

(pause)

When the third breath has gone, let your attention come to where you are. The surface beneath you. The room around you. The quality of the air. The temperature against your skin.

You are still in the threshold. The day has not quite released you. The night has not quite taken you. You are at the moment of crossing — the moment when the Mesektet is just beginning to move beneath you.

(pause)

Now let the threshold pass.

The vessel that carried you through the living hours is behind you. The vessel that will carry you through the dark is already moving. You do not need to board it — you have already boarded. You did so when you lay down. The crossing happens at the moment of release, and that moment has occurred.

You have entered the first hour.

(pause)

The territory is bounded. The corridor extends ahead. On either side of the river, the welcoming gods are present. They do not require you to know their names. They are here because the territory has its inhabitants, and these are the ones who meet what has just arrived.

You do not need to greet them. They are greeting you.

The light here is not the daylight you carried into the threshold. It is also not the deep dark of the further hours. It is the light of arrival — diminished, sufficient, the light by which the territory makes itself just visible enough for the passage to proceed.

(pause)

Notice what you have brought with you.

Not all of it. Most of what the day asked of you has been left at the threshold, where it belongs. But some weight remains — some last work of the living hours, some attention that has not yet released. The first hour does not require you to release it. The first hour only registers that it is here.

Let what remains be present without instruction.

(pause)

The barque is moving. You do not steer it. You do not need to attend to its course. The crew is at its stations. The defenders are in place. The deeper hours are ahead, but they are not yet.

What is happening now is arrival.

Something on the other side of the threshold has noted your presence. Something registers that you have entered the territory. You are not unobserved here. You are not alone here. You have arrived in a place that recognizes arrival.

(pause)

Let yourself be seen by what sees you.

This is the work of the first hour. Not transformation. Not dissolution. Not the deeper passage that will come in its own time. Only this: that you have crossed, that you are here, that the territory acknowledges what has entered it.

(longer pause)

The corridor continues. The barque proceeds. The first hour completes itself without your direction.

Now let your awareness soften.

You do not need to follow the barque. You do not need to track its progress. The crew is awake. The defenders are in position. The passage proceeds whether you observe it or not — and from here, you are not asked to observe.

You are asked to release.

(pause)

Let the corridor become indistinct. Let the welcoming gods recede into the territory they belong to. Let the river beneath the barque carry the vessel forward without you watching.

What remains is only your weight on the surface beneath you, your breath in your body, the dark behind your closed eyes.

The first hour is complete in you. You do not need to know when the second begins.

(pause)

If sleep is near, let it come. If it is not yet near, let your breath continue without instruction. Either is correct. The passage does not require your consciousness to proceed.

You have been registered. The territory knows you have arrived. The crew is awake.

Rest now.

The Second Hour

| *The night begins by feeding on what you brought.*

What the Amduat Describes

The second hour is the hour of **Wernes**, the field of the river of fire. The Mesektet has left the welcoming corridor of the first hour and entered a wider region — a fertile territory bisected by a great waterway. The river of fire runs through it. Vegetation grows on its banks. The inhabitants of Wernes are not the welcoming gods of the first hour but a different kind of presence: those who dwell in the field permanently, those who have crossed before and now live in the territory itself.

These are the *bau* of the blessed — the souls of those who completed earlier passages and now inhabit the Duat as permanent residents rather than travelers. They are not waiting for anything. They live here. The river of fire feeds them. The field sustains them. They are the population of the night.

Ra's function in this hour is distribution. As the barque moves through Wernes, the crew distributes provisions — bread, grain, the substance that sustains the dead. Hu speaks the names of what is given. Heka makes the giving effective. The inhabitants receive what the barque carries to them, and the barque continues, lighter for what it has given away.

The light here is dimmer than the first hour but not yet dark. Wernes is described in the *Amduat* with a particular fertility — green, watered, abundant — which is striking in a territory that is technically the underworld. The Duat is not barren. It has its own ecology. The second hour shows that ecology in its sustained form.

The Theological Claim

The second hour establishes a claim that contradicts almost every contemporary framework for understanding sleep: **the night feeds on what you bring into it.**

The modern account treats sleep as a recovery process — the body restoring itself, the mind discharging accumulated stress, the system returning to a baseline. The metaphor is depletion and replenishment. The day uses you up. The night refills you. What you carry into sleep is, in this account, the residue to be processed, the waste to be cleared, the noise to be quieted.

The barque tradition reverses this. What you carry into the night is not residue. It is provision. The inhabitants of the Duat — the *bau* of the blessed, the gods of the deeper hours, the forces that will work on you in the dissolution and reconstitution to come — feed on what the day produced in you. The encounters of the living hours, the work, the difficulties, the joys, the unfinished thoughts, the grief that wasn't fully addressed, the love that wasn't fully spoken — all of it becomes the substance the night metabolizes.

The early hours of sleep are the hours of provision. Before the dissolution at the fifth hour, before the confrontation at the seventh, before the reconstitution that begins after, the night first takes inventory of what arrived. It distributes that material across the territory it will need to work with. Wernes receives what was carried in. The inhabitants are fed. The deeper hours are stocked with what they will require.

This reframes the practitioner's relationship to what they carry into sleep entirely. The unresolved thought is not failure to clear the mind. It is provision for the night's work. The difficulty that the living hours could not resolve is not what you should have processed before bed. It is what the Mesektet is now distributing to those who can work with it. The barque cannot complete the deeper passage with nothing to work on. The day's content is what the night is for.

The Barque in This Hour

The Mesektet moves more deliberately through Wernes than it did through the corridor of the first hour. The crew is no longer at rest. Hu's voice is active — he is speaking the names of what is given, and each utterance places the provision with the inhabitant who can receive it. Heka makes the distribution effective; the giving is not symbolic but operative. Sia perceives where each thing belongs. Wepwawet has opened the wider field; the barque now moves through it.

Ra remains in the cabin, but the cabin is no longer closed. He is present to the distribution — not directing it, but acknowledging it. The provisions that are given come from him in the sense that he is the source of the passage that delivered them, but the work of distribution belongs to the crew.

Set, Mehen, Isis, and Nephthys are at their stations but the threat is still hours away. They observe the distribution. They do not interrupt it.

Practitioner Application

The second hour corresponds to the early dreams — the dream activity that begins as sleep deepens but before the dissolution of the fifth hour. The early-night dreams that often replay the day's content: encounters with people you saw, fragments of conversations, the textures of the spaces you moved through, the unresolved thoughts that the living hours did not finish.

These dreams are often dismissed in contemporary frameworks as the mind processing residue. The barque tradition names what is actually happening: provision is being distributed. The day's content is being placed where it can be worked with. The dreams are the visible surface of the territory receiving what the barque brought.

This means that the second hour's dreams have a different character than the dreams of the deeper hours. They are not yet symbolic in the way that deep dreams become symbolic. They are not yet the communications of Morpheus that Greek tradition identified. They are the early metabolism — the day being placed into the night's keeping.

You do not need to remember these dreams to benefit from the hour. The metabolism proceeds whether or not you witness it. But practitioners who do wake briefly in the early hours of sleep, or who notice dream-fragments as they drift in and out of the first stages of rest, are seeing the second hour at its work. The fragments are not noise. They are distribution.

In the **acknowledgment register**, the practitioner who notices the early-night dreams can recognize: *The day is being distributed. The night is feeding on what I carried in. The provision is happening.*

In the **devotional register**, the practitioner can offer: *Inhabitants of Wernes, receive what the day produced. Let it nourish what dwells here. Let it become the substance the deeper hours will require.*

The hour does not ask for more than this.

A Guided Meditation for the Second Hour

For use as the practitioner moves into the early stages of sleep, or as a deliberate practice on a night when the second hour is to be inhabited consciously.

If you are still awake, settle further. The first hour is behind you. The territory has registered your arrival. Now something else begins.

(pause)

Let your body release any last holding. The threshold has been crossed. The corridor of the first hour has opened into a wider region. You are moving now through Wernes — the fertile field, the river of fire, the territory that lives.

(pause)

Notice what you have brought into this region. Not the things you tried to release at the threshold — those are gone, or they will be. What remains. The textures of the day that did not finish dissolving. The faces you saw. The conversations you carried in. The small unresolved problems. The love and the difficulty that the living hours did not exhaust.

You do not need to hold any of it consciously. You only need to know it is here, in you, in the barque.

(pause)

The crew is distributing what you brought.

Hu is speaking the names of what is being given. Heka is making the distribution effective. The inhabitants of Wernes are receiving the provisions — the *bau* of the blessed, the souls who live here permanently, the gods who dwell in this region of the night. They are being fed by what your day produced.

(pause)

Let this be enough.

You do not need to participate in the distribution. You do not need to direct what is given to whom. The crew knows. The inhabitants know. Hu names what is given, and the name places the provision correctly. Heka makes the giving real. Sia perceives where each thing belongs.

What you do is allow the distribution to proceed.

(longer pause)

The barque is lighter now. What you carried in has been received. The provisions have been placed where they will be needed in the deeper hours. The night has been fed.

(pause)

Now let the awareness of the distribution recede. You do not need to follow the barque any further into Wernes. The hour is completing itself. The river of fire continues to flow. The inhabitants continue to receive. None of it requires your conscious attention.

(pause)

What remains in you is only your weight, your breath, the dark behind your closed eyes. The second hour is complete in you. You do not need to know when the third begins.

If sleep is deepening, let it deepen. If you remain on the edge of it, let the edge hold you. Either is correct.

The provisions are placed. The night has what it needs.

Rest now.

The Third Hour

The dead are not far. You pass through their territory every night.

What the Amduat Describes

The third hour deepens into a region the *Amduat* calls the *field of the* bau *of the dead*, or sometimes the field of Osiris-in-his-power. The Mesektet has left the bright fertility of Wernes and entered darker territory. The river runs differently here. The vegetation is sparser. The light is more diminished. And the population has changed.

The inhabitants of this hour are the dead in their organized form. They are arranged in three registers — three bands of population running parallel to the barque's passage — and each register has its own character, its own gates, its own requirements. The blessed dead are here, but so are the dead who are still being sorted, and so are those who serve Osiris's authority in this region.

This is the first hour where Osiris's presence becomes substantial. He himself remains in the deeper hours — the still center of the fifth is where he is most fully encountered — but his power extends into this third hour. The territory bears his name. The dead organized in their registers acknowledge his authority. The Mesektet passes through regions where he is the structural presence even if he is not yet visibly at work.

The crew's function in this hour is recognition. Hu speaks the names of the dead as the barque passes. Each named one is acknowledged. The dead, in turn, recognize Ra — they look up from their stations and register that the solar god is moving through their territory. The recognition is mutual and required. A barque that did not speak the names would be unrecognized by the inhabitants; a population that did not acknowledge Ra would fail in its function within the Duat's structure.

Wepwawet is active in this hour. The way through the field of the dead is not single — the registers branch, the gates multiply, and the path that the Mesektet takes requires specific opening. Wepwawet identifies which way through this hour belongs to this night's passage. Different nights move through the field of the dead by different routes.

The Theological Claim

The third hour establishes a claim the contemporary reader is most likely to resist: **the dead are present in the territory the night crosses, and the practitioner passes through their region every night.**

This is not a claim about memory. Memory is a function of the living mind, an act the practitioner performs by recalling someone who has died. The third hour is the inverse: not the living recalling the dead, but the night carrying the practitioner through a region where the dead live. The passage is from the practitioner's side. The dead are already there.

The Egyptian frame is explicit about this. The *bau* of the dead are not figures in a dream-landscape projected by the sleeping mind. They are residents of the Duat — the territory the barque crosses — and the Duat is real in the same way the visible world is real. The night is structured. The structure includes its inhabitants. The inhabitants include those who have died.

The Greek frame arrives at the same conclusion through different language. Hypnos and Thanatos are brothers. They are not opposites; they are kin. Every night that you cross through Hypnos's domain, you are crossing through a territory adjacent to his brother's. The Greeks did not separate these. They understood sleep as a small death — temporary, but structurally identical to the larger crossing, and located in the same region of reality.

This is the hour where the practitioner meets, structurally, what most contemporary frameworks insist on locating elsewhere. The dead are not in a separate place reached only by the formal ritual of dying. They are present in the territory the night crosses, and you cross that territory every night, and the crossing is itself a recognition.

You do not need to know the dead by name. You do not need to have any specific relationship to anyone who has died. The recognition is structural rather than personal: the territory contains the dead, and the barque passes through, and the passage acknowledges what is there. Some nights you will dream of someone you knew who has died. Some nights you will not. The third hour proceeds regardless. The dead are population of the night whether or not they appear in your dreams.

This is the theological pivot of the early hours. Hour I established that the territory acknowledges your arrival. Hour II established that the night feeds on what you bring. Hour III establishes that the territory you cross contains the dead, and the crossing is itself a form of being among them.

The Barque in This Hour

The Mesektet moves carefully through the field of the dead. The crew is alert in a different way than they were in Wernes — there, the work was distribution; here, the work is recognition. Hu speaks more in this hour than in the previous two. His utterances name what the barque passes, and each name maintains the relationship between the solar order and the order of the dead.

Wepwawet has more to do in this hour than in any of the previous. The way through the three registers requires choice — which gate, which sequence, which approach. The path is not given automatically. Wepwawet finds the one that belongs to this night's passage and opens it.

Ra remains in the cabin, but his function has shifted. He is no longer simply being carried; he is being recognized. The dead look up as the barque passes. The barque returns the recognition. This is exchange, not transit. The relationship between the solar order and the order of the dead is maintained at every passage and the third hour is where the maintenance happens.

Set, Mehen, Isis, and Nephthys remain at their stations. The threat is still hours away. But Nephthys, in particular, attends closely in this hour — her mourning, her function of holding the dissolution as sacred, has begun to be needed even before the fifth hour. The field of the dead is her territory in a way the previous two hours were not. She is among kin here.

Practitioner Application

The third hour corresponds to the sleep that has deepened past the early dreams of Hour II but has not yet reached the dissolution of the fifth. This is the territory where dreams of the dead occur — when they occur. The dream of the parent who died, the dream of the friend who died, the dream of someone the practitioner barely knew but who has died and now appears: these dreams have their location, and the location is the third hour.

The practitioner who has dreamed of the dead and woken disoriented, uncertain how to receive the dream, is meeting the third hour without a framework. Was the dream a visit? A projection? A memory the sleeping mind constructed? The contemporary frames have no clean answer because they begin from the assumption that the dead are elsewhere. The barque tradition begins from a different assumption: the dead are population of the night, and the practitioner crosses their territory regularly, and the dream of the dead is the surface manifestation of a crossing that happens whether dreams arrive or not.

This does not require the practitioner to believe anything specific about what happens after death. The Duat is a territory of the dead in the *Amduat*'s account; it is not a theological account of what dying means for the individual. What it asserts is that the territory exists, that the dead are present in it, and that the night carries you through it. What you do with that knowledge — what relationship you cultivate to the dead you encounter, what you make of the dreams that come from this hour — is yours to develop. The hour itself proceeds without requiring your interpretive framework.

In the **acknowledgment register**, the practitioner who notices a dream of the dead, or who simply settles into the deeper hours of sleep, can recognize: *I am crossing the field of the dead. They are here. The barque acknowledges them. I am carried through their region.*

In the **devotional register**, the practitioner can offer: *Dead of the third hour, I pass through your territory. I do not know your names. I acknowledge that you are here. Receive my passage as I acknowledge your residence.*

There is one further thing the third hour suggests, and it is worth letting land carefully. The dead the practitioner specifically loved — those whose loss is carried in the body — are not strangers to this hour. They are among the population. Some nights they will be in the path of the barque. Some nights they will not. The practitioner who has lost someone and who occasionally dreams of them is not having a coincidence. The third hour is where such dreams come from. They are visits within a territory that contains both the practitioner and the dead, briefly, while the passage permits it.

You do not summon these dreams. You do not direct them. You can only acknowledge that the territory of the third hour exists and that you cross it, and that the dead you loved are not as far as the living world insists they are.

A Guided Meditation for the Third Hour

For use as the practitioner moves into deeper sleep, or as a deliberate practice on a night when the third hour is to be inhabited consciously.

The first hour received you. The second fed the territory on what you brought. Now something deeper.

(pause)

Let your body settle past the early stages. The corridor and the fertile field are behind you. The barque has entered a region the river runs through differently — darker, more populated, organized in ways the earlier hours were not.

(pause)

You are passing through the field of the dead.

This is not frightening unless you make it so. The dead are not waiting to take you. They are not hostile. They are residents of the territory the night crosses, organized in their registers, attending to their own work, raising their eyes only briefly as the barque moves by.

(pause)

The crew is doing the work of recognition. Hu speaks the names of those who require naming. The dead acknowledge the passage. The passage acknowledges the dead. None of this requires your active participation. The exchange happens whether you witness it or not.

(pause)

You may notice, in the third hour, that someone you knew who has died is present in the territory. They do not appear because you summoned them. They appear because the barque is passing through their region and you happen to be on the barque. The proximity is structural.

If you sense them, you do not need to do anything. You do not need to speak to them. You do not need to receive a message. You only need to recognize that they are here, in this region, and that the night has brought you close to them, briefly, as it brings every practitioner close to their dead in this hour.

(longer pause)

Let the recognition be enough.

The barque continues. The field of the dead extends in three registers around the vessel. Wepwawet has chosen the way through. The crew is doing its work. The dead are doing theirs. You are being carried, recognized, brought near and then past.

(pause)

Whatever you encountered here will go with you into the deeper hours, or it will remain in this region. Either is correct. You do not need to hold what was offered. You do not need to release it. The territory will manage what belongs to the territory.

(pause)

Now let the awareness of the third hour recede. The dead remain in their region. You continue forward into the territory ahead. The fourth hour is the difficult passage — the realm of Sokar, where the barque must be towed — but that is not yet. The third hour is completing itself first.

(pause)

What remains in you is only your weight, your breath, the dark behind your closed eyes. The third hour is complete in you. The dead have been acknowledged. The passage continues.

You will not remember most of what happened in this region. You are not meant to. The recognition was real. The fragments you carry forward — if any come — are the gift of the hour, not its purpose.

Rest now.

The barque is moving.

The Fourth Hour

The river ends. The barque is dragged. The night becomes work.

What the Amduat Describes

The fourth hour brings the barque to **Rosetau**, the realm of Sokar. The territory changes more sharply here than at any prior threshold of the passage. The river that has carried the Mesektet since dusk runs dry. The water that has been the barque's medium since the western horizon ends. What lies ahead is sand.

The Mesektet cannot travel on sand. A vessel built for water has no native means of moving across the dry terrain of Sokar's realm. The *Amduat* depicts what happens next with unusual precision: the barque is fitted with ropes. Gods take up positions at the prow and along the sides. The vessel is dragged across the sand by the labor of the crew and by additional deities who have come to assist with the difficult passage.

The territory is not only dry but corridored. Rosetau is a region of narrow passages cut through stone, guarded at intervals by serpents who must be driven back to permit transit. These are not Apophis — the great serpent of uncreation is still hours away — but lesser serpents, territorial presences whose function is to make the passage of Sokar's realm difficult for any traveler. Set's spear engages here, briefly, on each one. The serpents withdraw. The corridor opens. The barque is dragged forward.

Sokar himself dwells at the heart of this region. He is depicted in the *Amduat* as falcon-headed, hawk-eyed, standing on the back of a great serpent who is contained rather than driven back. Sokar is not hostile to the passage, but he is not welcoming in the way the inhabitants of Wernes were welcoming. He is the deep god of the mineral earth, of the territory where solar light has the hardest time penetrating, and the Mesektet must pass through his realm without his active assistance. He observes. He permits. He does not help.

The light in this hour is the dimmest yet. The fertility of Wernes is gone. The organized population of the third hour's field of the dead is behind. What remains is rock, sand, narrow passages, the dwelling-place of a god who does not trade. The barque moves forward only because the crew drags it.

The Theological Claim

The fourth hour establishes what the previous three did not need to: **the passage is sometimes hard.**

Hours I, II, and III each had their own quality, but none of them required labor. The crew functioned, the territory received, the dead were acknowledged, and the barque moved forward as a matter of course. The fourth hour ends that easy movement. The river runs dry. The vessel that was carried must now be dragged. The territory itself resists the passage, and the resistance is structural rather than incidental.

This is the hour the contemporary reader most needs and most resists. The reader has been promised — by every framework that approaches the night as restoration, sleep as recovery, the dark as nurturing — that the night should feel a particular way. Soft. Restful. Easy. The fourth hour contradicts that promise without apology. Some hours of the passage are simply hard. The territory of Rosetau is dry and corridored and serpent-guarded, and the crossing of it requires labor that the earlier hours did not.

The fourth hour does not contain a crisis. There is no Apophis attack here — that is hours away. There is no dissolution at the still center — that is also hours away. What there is, is the simple fact that the night has reached a region where movement is not given. The crew must work. The serpents must be driven back. The corridors must be opened one at a time. None of this is wrong. None of this is failure. It is what the fourth hour is.

The implication for the practitioner is structural rather than instructional. You will sometimes find that the night has stopped being easy. The hours have passed and you are no longer in the corridor of arrival or the fertile field of distribution. You are somewhere drier and harder. Sleep itself feels like work, or you wake briefly in the deep hours with a sense that the night is laboring, or the morning brings a tiredness that is not solved by more hours of sleep. The fourth hour is doing this. The territory has changed. The crossing is requiring more.

This does not mean the practitioner has done something wrong. It does not mean the practice is failing. It means the passage has reached Rosetau, where every barque labors, every night that any human has ever slept. The fourth hour is not personal. It is structural.

The relief in this — if relief is the right word — is that the labor is the crew's, not yours. You are not being asked to drag the vessel. You are being carried, even when the carrying has become difficult. The work of Hour IV belongs to the gods who pull the ropes and the gods who drive back the serpents and the god whose realm permits the passage. You are present in the cabin, undergoing what is being done on your behalf. The labor is real. The labor is also not yours.

The Barque in This Hour

The Mesektet has changed. It is no longer the vessel gliding through water of the earlier hours. It is being dragged — visibly, materially — across terrain that resists it.

The crew has multiplied in this hour. Sia and Hu and Heka and Wepwawet and the steersman remain, but they are joined by additional gods who have come to help with the towing. The *Amduat* shows them at the ropes, pulling, straining. The work is depicted without idealization. Even gods labor at the fourth hour.

Set is most active here that he has been so far in the passage. The serpents of Rosetau are not the great enemy, but they are real obstacles, and Set drives each one back. His spear is in use. His ferocity is engaged. The reader who carries the modern association of Set with villainy will need to set that aside in this hour. He is doing necessary work. The passage continues because he does it.

Mehen remains coiled around the cabin. Ra remains within. His diminished form is most apparent in this hour because the territory itself reduces him — the dry corridors of Sokar's realm do not feed solar presence the way the open fields of the earlier hours did. He is ram-headed here, aged, fully enclosed. He is being protected because he is most vulnerable.

Isis and Nephthys do magical work that does not show. The sustained protection of the passage's integrity becomes harder in Rosetau, where the surrounding territory does not contribute to the crossing. They speak. The structure holds. The barque is dragged forward across the sand.

Practitioner Application

The fourth hour corresponds to the deep hours of the night when sleep has stopped being restorative in the simple sense. The 2 AM waking. The 3 AM waking. The brief surfacing into consciousness during what should be the most consolidated stretch of sleep. The morning that begins with the feeling that the night was working hard even though nothing specific can be named about it.

These experiences are not failures of the practice. They are not signs that the practitioner has slept badly, or has unprocessed material, or has failed to release the day at the threshold. They are the fourth hour. The territory of Rosetau is genuinely difficult to cross, and a practitioner whose passage moves through this territory each night may sometimes feel that the night is laboring.

What changes when the practitioner has this framework is not the experience itself. The fourth hour will remain what it is — the river runs dry, the barque is dragged, the corridors are opened one at a time — regardless of how the practitioner understands it. What changes is the practitioner's relationship to it. The 3 AM waking that previously felt like personal failure becomes, with this framework, the fourth hour briefly surfacing into awareness. The morning tiredness that previously felt like evidence of doing sleep wrong becomes, with this framework, the recognition that the night did real work in territory that resists easy crossing.

There are practitioners whose lives are passing through extended fourth-hour territory. The grief that does not lift quickly. The illness that exhausts. The vocational struggle that does not resolve. The relationship that is dissolving slowly. These are not failures of the daily passage — they are the longer fourth hours of a life, where the river of the easier seasons has run dry and the labor of the crossing has become more visible. The barque continues. The crew still functions. But the night, in these seasons, will sometimes feel like work in a way that the seasons of the fertile field did not.

The practice for the fourth hour is simple and demanding: you do not need to do anything. The crew is doing the labor. The serpents are being driven back. The corridors are opening. Sokar permits the passage. Your task is what it has always been: to be on the vessel, to consent to the crossing, to allow what is happening on your behalf to happen.

When the night feels hard, the night is sometimes simply hard. The fourth hour does not require your interpretation or your repair. It requires your continued presence in the cabin while the dragging is done.

In the **acknowledgment register**, the practitioner who finds themselves awake in the deep hours, or who notices that the night has stopped being easy, can recognize: *I am at Rosetau. The river has run dry. The barque is being dragged. The labor is the crew's. I am being carried through.*

In the **devotional register**, the practitioner can offer: *Crew of the fourth hour, you drag the barque across the sand. Sokar, you permit the passage. Set, you drive back what would obstruct it. I do not know how to thank you for this labor. I acknowledge that it is being done.*

The hour asks nothing further.

A Guided Meditation for the Fourth Hour

For use as the practitioner moves into the deep hours of the night, or as a deliberate practice on a night when the fourth hour is to be inhabited consciously — especially if the practitioner has been waking in the deep hours and wishes to meet that waking with a framework.

The third hour is behind you. The field of the dead has been crossed. The barque has moved into deeper territory.

(pause)

Notice that something has changed in the quality of the passage. The earlier hours had their own ease — the welcoming corridor, the fertile field, the recognition of the dead. This hour is different.

(pause)

The river that carried the barque has ended. The territory ahead is dry. The Mesektet that has been gliding through water since the threshold is now being fitted with ropes. The crew is taking positions at the prow and the sides. Additional gods have come to help with the labor.

The barque is being dragged.

(pause)

You are not being asked to pull. You have never been asked to pull. The crew labors because the crew is what labors. Your position remains what it has been — in the cabin, in your diminished form, being carried through.

But you may feel the change in the vessel. The smooth movement of the earlier hours has become something else. The barque advances now in pulls, in pauses, in the labor of dragging. Mehen has tightened his coils around the cabin because the territory has become harder. Set's spear is active because the serpents of Rosetau must be driven back. Isis and Nephthys are speaking what holds the passage together.

(pause)

This is not wrong. This is the fourth hour.

(longer pause)

If you have been waking in the deep hours of the night, you may be feeling something now of what the barque feels. The sense that the night has stopped being easy. The labor without a name. The crossing that is requiring more.

You do not need to interpret it. You do not need to repair it. You do not need to release whatever you suspect might be blocking the easier passage of the earlier hours. There is no blockage. The fourth hour is structurally difficult. Every barque labors here. Every practitioner who has ever passed through this territory has met the place where the river runs dry.

(pause)

Let yourself be carried even through the labor.

The crew is at the ropes. The serpents are being driven back. Sokar observes from his stone throne and permits the passage. The barque is moving — slowly, against resistance, but moving. The corridors are opening one at a time.

What you are asked to do is what you have always been asked to do: nothing. Remain in the cabin. Allow the dragging to occur. Allow the labor that belongs to the gods to be the gods' labor.

(pause)

If you remain awake within this meditation rather than returning to sleep, this is not a failure. The fourth hour sometimes surfaces practitioners into consciousness. You may be briefly in Nyx's household, awake within the territory of Rosetau, witnessing what is usually done while you sleep.

Do not perform. Do not strive. Do not try to make sense of why the night has become work. The work is structural. You are present in it because the night brought you here, and the night will carry you forward when the next hour begins.

(pause)

The fifth hour is ahead — the still center, the tomb of Osiris, the moment of deepest dissolution and the beginning of reconstitution. But that is not yet. The fourth hour is completing itself first. The barque is being dragged through the last corridor of Rosetau. The serpents have been driven back. The crew is straining at the ropes.

(pause)

Let what remains in you be only your weight, your breath, the dark behind your closed eyes. The fourth hour is complete in you. The labor was done on your behalf. The territory is being crossed.

You will not remember most of what occurred here. You are not meant to. The crossing was real. The morning, when it comes, will carry the trace of this labor even if you cannot name it.

Rest now.

The barque is being dragged forward.

The Fifth Hour

> The barque stops. The merging occurs. Nothing in you is what it was.

What the Amduat Describes

The fourth hour ends. The barque emerges from the last corridor of Rosetau into a wider chamber. The labor of dragging is complete. The crew sets down the ropes. The vessel comes to rest.

This is the **cavern of Sokar**, the deepest interior of the Duat. The chamber is not lit. The only light is what Ra himself still carries within his diminished form, and that light is at its lowest. The walls of the chamber are stone. The floor is sand. The ceiling rises into a darkness the eye cannot measure.

At the center of the chamber is a burial mound. The *Amduat* depicts it as a low rise of earth, perfectly formed, motionless. Above the mound is an oval — described in some recensions as the night sky compressed, in others as the boundary of what is being held within. Inside the oval is the body of Osiris in his death. Not Osiris alive, not Osiris reigning, not Osiris-in-his-power as the third hour invoked him. Osiris in the stillness of his own dissolution, awaiting what will be done.

Below the mound, in the deeper representations, is the head of Sokar — the same falcon-headed god from the previous hour, but now shown as if fused with the underworld itself. Sokar's head is the foundation. Osiris's body is what rests above it. The mound is the structure of the still center.

The crew of the Mesektet attends. Hu does not speak in this hour. Sia perceives but his perception is silent. Wepwawet stands at his station without opening any way, because no way needs to be opened yet — the territory ahead has not yet been arranged. The steersman holds the tiller of a stationary vessel. Set's spear is not in use; the serpents of the previous hour are behind, and Apophis is not yet ahead. Mehen's coils remain around the cabin but their tension has changed — the protection is no longer against external threat but around what is about to occur.

What occurs is the descent.

Ra's *ba* — his soul, the essential aspect of him that is not the visible form — leaves the cabin. It descends from the barque into the burial mound. It enters the oval where Osiris's body waits. And there, in the deepest interior of the deepest hour, the *ba* of Ra and the body of Osiris merge.

This is the still center.

It is not depicted with drama in the *Amduat*. There is no narrative climax. The merging is shown as fact: the *ba* enters, the body receives, the two become briefly one. The text describes this with the same precision it uses for the geography of the corridors and the names of the inhabitants. The merging is what the fifth hour is for.

After the merging — the *Amduat* does not specify how long it lasts, because the question does not apply — the *ba* of Ra rises again. It returns to the barque. The crew receives it. The vessel begins, very slowly, to move forward again. The cavern of Sokar is behind. The sixth hour begins.

The Theological Claim

The fifth hour is the claim that organizes the entire Duat: **the practitioner is taken apart and put back together, briefly, in the deepest interior of the night.**

Everything else in the Duat material — the vessel and the crew, the defenders and the dead, the labor of Rosetau and the reconstitution that follows — exists in relation to this hour. Hour V is what the rest of the passage is organized around. Without the merging, the night would be transit. With the merging, the night is renewal.

What happens at the still center is not symbolic processing. It is not the mind sorting the day. It is the structural event in which what you are is dissolved into a larger pattern, briefly, and reconstituted from that pattern before consciousness returns. The merging of Ra and Osiris is the cosmological act by which renewal becomes possible at all. Without that act repeated each night, the sun would not rise. Without the practitioner's equivalent of that act repeated each night, the practitioner would not wake.

This is why the fifth hour is dreamless. The territory cannot be witnessed by the conscious mind because the conscious mind is precisely what must be suspended for the merging to occur. The *ba* cannot descend if the ego is monitoring. The body of Osiris cannot receive what arrives if the practitioner is watching to see what is being received. The still center is structurally inaccessible to awareness. The hour proceeds without you.

You do not remember the fifth hour. You will never remember the fifth hour. Every night you sleep fully, you pass through it, and every morning you wake without any memory of having been there. The forgetting is not failure of recall. It is the condition of the hour. What happened in the cavern of Sokar happened in you, but it happened in a region of you that consciousness does not reach.

What you may notice, in the morning, is the trace. The clarity that was not available the night before. The weight that has been set down without your conscious effort. The knowing that arrived during the dark. The unraveling of something that the living hours had been holding too tightly. These are the surface signs of what the fifth hour did. The act itself remains hidden.

The implication is theological and practical at once. Theologically: you are not a continuous self crossing nights without alteration. You are something that comes apart and is put back together every twenty-four hours, and the coming-apart-and-being-put-back-together is what allows you to continue. Practically: the fifth hour is what you trust. You consent to it at the threshold without knowing what will happen there, and you wake from it with what it produced, and the consenting and the receiving are the entirety of your participation. The hour belongs to Ra and Osiris and the cavern of Sokar. You are present in it without knowing you are present in it.

This is the hour the rest of the practice exists to protect.

The Barque in This Hour

The Mesektet has stopped. For the first and only time in the twelve hours of the passage, the vessel is not moving. The crew is at their stations but they are not performing the active functions that have defined the previous hours. The barque has come to rest because the work of this hour is not motion. It is the merging that happens at the still center, and that merging requires the vessel to be present rather than passing.

Ra is in his most diminished form. The cabin holds him fully — Mehen's coils are at their tightest — and his *ba* has departed downward. What remains in the cabin is the body of Ra without his vital essence, the form without its animating presence. This is the closest the solar god comes to his own death, and the closest the practitioner comes to theirs.

The crew attends in silence. The defenders attend in silence. Even Isis and Nephthys, whose magical work usually maintains the structure of the passage, have nothing to speak in this hour. The structure holds itself. The merging proceeds. The cavern receives.

This is what stillness is, in the *Amduat's* sense: not the absence of activity, but the form of activity in which presence replaces movement. Everything is happening. Nothing is moving. The hour completes itself in this paradox.

Practitioner Application

The fifth hour corresponds to the dreamless deep sleep that occurs in the middle hours of the night. Biological frameworks call this slow-wave sleep, deep sleep, or stage three NREM. The cosmological frame names it differently: it is the hour when the practitioner passes through the cavern of Sokar, and the merging occurs in them.

You do not remember it. You are not meant to. The practitioner who is concerned that they do not remember their deep sleep is, without knowing it, asking for the wrong thing. The fifth hour cannot be remembered because consciousness is suspended for it. The forgetting is the condition of the hour proceeding correctly. If you remembered the still center, the still center would not have occurred.

What can be noticed is the trace at dawn. The morning that arrives with something altered. The shift that cannot be located in a specific thought or feeling but is felt as a change in the ground of how you are. The grief that has loosened slightly. The decision that became clear without effort. The capacity for the day that was not there the night before. These are the surface signs of the merging. The hour produced them in you.

The implication for daily practice is the Midnight Passage, which is the threshold rite the original eight foundational chapters already established. The Pre-Sleep Acknowledgment is the act by which you offer your conscious participation in the fifth hour before consciousness is taken from you. The Waking-Night Rite is what is available if you find yourself briefly surfaced in Nyx's household during the deep hours adjacent to this one. Both rites point toward the fifth hour without entering it. They acknowledge what they cannot witness.

The implication beyond daily practice is harder. There are passages in a life that are equivalent to extended fifth hours — periods of months or years in which the practitioner is being dissolved and reconstituted at a depth they cannot witness. These are not the longer fourth hours of grief and illness and vocational struggle, where the labor is visible. The longer fifth hours are quieter and harder to name. They are the seasons of a life in which something fundamental is being reorganized in the practitioner without their conscious participation, and the only sign is the eventual recognition that they are not who they were when the season began.

If you have come through such a season — or if you are inside one — the cavern of Sokar is your structural location. The merging is occurring. You will not be able to witness it. You will only be able to consent to it, and to recognize, eventually, that something has been done in you that you did not direct.

In the **acknowledgment register**, the practitioner can recognize: *The still center is where I am taken apart and put back together. I will not see it. I trust that it is occurring.*

In the **devotional register**, the practitioner can offer: *Osiris, you receive what descends. Ra, you descend. The merging proceeds whether I witness it or not. I consent to what is being done in me at the still center.*

The hour itself does not need your participation. It needs your consent at the threshold and your acknowledgment of the trace at dawn. These are sufficient.

A Guided Meditation for the Fifth Hour

This meditation is shorter than those of the previous hours because the fifth hour is shorter in what it asks of awareness. The practitioner

> *cannot meditate inside the still center; the still center suspends
> meditation along with everything else. What follows is meditation at
> the threshold of the merging — the consent that immediately precedes
> the hour you will not witness.*

The fourth hour is behind you. The labor of Rosetau is complete. The barque has been dragged through the last corridor and into a wider chamber.

(pause)

The chamber is still. The ropes have been set down. The crew has come to rest. The vessel is no longer moving.

(pause)

You have arrived at the cavern of Sokar.

The chamber holds, at its center, a burial mound. Above the mound is an oval that contains the body of Osiris in his death. Below the mound is the deeper foundation of the underworld itself. This is what the entire passage has been moving toward.

(pause)

What is about to occur cannot be witnessed.

In a moment, Ra's *ba* will leave the barque and descend into the mound. It will enter the oval. It will merge with the body of Osiris. The merging is the still center. It is what the night is for.

You will not see it. You cannot follow it. The merging is the hour your consciousness does not reach.

(longer pause)

What is asked of you here is consent.

Not active consent, not effortful consent — only the willingness to be present in the cabin while the *ba* descends and returns. You do not have to direct anything. You do not have to understand anything. You only have to permit what is about to be done on your behalf.

If you sleep fully tonight, this hour will occur in you. If you do not — if the fifth hour does not reach you tonight — it will occur on another night when sleep is full. It always occurs. Every practitioner who has ever fully slept has passed through it. The cavern is structural.

(pause)

Now release the meditation.

The hour ahead cannot be inhabited consciously. What you do now is what has been asked at every threshold of this passage: you board the vessel, you consent to the crossing, and you allow what is being done to be done. The crew attends in silence. The defenders attend in silence. The cavern of Sokar receives what is about to descend.

(pause)

Let your awareness soften further than at any previous hour.

The merging is beginning. You will not witness it. You will wake from it, eventually, carrying what it produced. Until then, the cavern holds the work, and the work proceeds, and you are present in it by being absent to it.

Rest now.

What the still center does, the still center does.

The Sixth Hour

Your dissolved self meets what is waiting for you in the deep water.

What the Amduat Describes

The cavern of Sokar opens. The barque, stationary through the entire still center, begins to move again — slowly, almost imperceptibly at first. The crew has resumed function. The ropes that dragged the vessel through Rosetau have been set aside. The barque is back in water.

The territory of the sixth hour is the **deep waters** — not the river that carried the Mesektet through the earlier hours, but a wider, stiller body. The water is dark. The depth is not described in the *Amduat* because the depth is not the point; what matters is that the territory holds something the previous hours did not.

At the center of the deep waters, the *Amduat* shows a figure. It is the body of Ra — not Ra-as-traveler, not Ra-in-his-diminished-form, not Ra-as-passenger-of-the-barque, but Ra's *body* as a separate aspect, lying in the water, awaiting what is about to occur. The body is undisturbed. The water does not move around it. It has been waiting through the entire passage so far for what only now can happen.

Surrounding the body are twelve gods. The *Amduat* names them as the Twelve Gods of the Deep, and their function in this hour is precise: they witness. They do not act. They do not lift the body or arrange it or speak over it. They are present at the perimeter of what is about to occur, holding the territory in which it becomes possible.

What occurs is the meeting.

Ra's *ba* — having ascended from the burial mound at the close of the fifth hour, having merged with Osiris there and returned changed — descends now toward the body in the deep water. The descent is not the same as the descent at the still center. There, the *ba* entered the burial mound and became one with Osiris. Here, the *ba* approaches the body, but the two do not merge. They meet. The *ba* hovers above the body, or beside it in some recensions, and the encounter is sustained without being fused.

This is the reconstitution beginning. The *ba* has been altered by the merging with Osiris. The body has been waiting through the passage for the *ba* to return in this altered form. What the sixth hour does is bring them into proximity — not yet into the single reanimated form that will be Khepri at the eastern horizon, but into the relationship from which that form will eventually be assembled.

The twelve gods attend. The water holds. The barque moves slowly across the deep, witnessing what is happening at its center. The hour ends with the *ba* and the body still in proximity, the reconstitution begun but unfinished.

The Theological Claim

The sixth hour establishes the claim the entire reconstitution arc depends on: **what was dissolved meets what was waiting.**

The fifth hour took the practitioner apart. The merging at the still center was real, and what was dissolved was not what the day-self imagined could be dissolved without consequence. The *ba* that descended into the burial mound is not the *ba* that ascended from it. Something was altered in the merging. Something was integrated from Osiris that was not present in Ra before the descent. The *ba* that returns to the surface of the deep waters in the sixth hour is the *ba* of a god who has been changed.

The body, meanwhile, has been waiting.

This is the most easily missed part of the theology. The body is not dead in the sense of inert matter awaiting reanimation. The body is in a specific state — the state of having been left behind when the *ba* descended, the state of holding the form of Ra during the dissolution, the state of remaining itself across the still center while the *ba* underwent its merging. The body is the continuity. It is what allows the reconstitution to be reconstitution rather than replacement. Without a body that remained itself through the merging, what returned at dawn would be a new god, not the same god altered. The body's waiting is what allows the altered *ba* to come home rather than to arrive somewhere unfamiliar.

This applies to the practitioner. What is taken apart at the still center is real, and what is altered there is also real. But you wake as yourself. The continuity you experience at dawn — the sense that you are the same person who fell asleep, even though something in you has shifted — is the work of the body. The body waited. The dissolved *ba* met it again in the deep waters. The proximity of that meeting is what makes the reconstituted form recognizable to you when consciousness returns.

This is also why grief sometimes feels the way it feels in the early morning. The waking that arrives carrying grief is often a waking in which the body has met an altered *ba*, and the *ba* has returned from a merging in which something was let go of that the body did not know was being let go. The body recognizes itself but does not recognize what the *ba* has become. The misalignment is brief — by the time the living hours have begun in earnest, the reconstitution has continued far enough that the body and the *ba* are no longer experienced as separate — but in those first minutes of morning, the gap is sometimes felt.

The sixth hour is the hour of this gap. This is what reconstitution looks like at its beginning.

The implication is theological and intimate at once. You are not, in the deepest sense, a single self crossing nights. You are a *ba* and a body whose relationship is sustained across the passage by the body's waiting and the *ba*'s return. When the relationship works smoothly — most nights — you do not notice the separation and reunion. When the relationship is briefly visible — in the gap-feeling of certain mornings, in the disorientation of waking from particularly deep sleep, in the strange tenderness of being newly reassembled before the day has fully claimed you — you are experiencing the sixth hour completing itself in you.

The Barque in This Hour

The Mesektet has begun moving again. Slowly. The water is deeper here than in the earlier hours, and the barque sits low in it. The crew is at their stations and active for the first time since the cavern, but their activity is muted. Hu is speaking, but his voice is quieter — the names he speaks are the names of the gods of the deep, and these names do not require the volume of the earlier hours' announcements. The gods being named are already present; the naming is acknowledgment, not summoning.

Sia perceives the meeting at the center of the deep waters. He does not narrate what he perceives. The crew is aware of what is occurring at the heart of the hour, and the awareness is enough.

Wepwawet has opened the way out of the cavern. The vessel travels through the deep waters along a path he has identified, but the path is broad here — the deep waters are wide, and the vessel can move across them in many directions, and Wepwawet has chosen the direction that brings the barque past the meeting of *ba* and body so that the crew can attend.

Ra remains in the cabin. This is important. Ra-as-passenger is in the cabin even while the *ba* of Ra is in the water meeting the body of Ra. The Egyptian theology of multiplicity allows for this — Ra is in several aspects at once, and the *Amduat* depicts these aspects simultaneously. The Ra in the cabin is the form being carried; the *ba* of Ra is the aspect that descended and is now returning; the body of Ra is what waited in the deep water. All three are Ra. None of them is the whole of Ra. The reconstitution is the bringing of these aspects into a relationship from which the whole can be assembled.

Set, Mehen, Isis, and Nephthys remain attentive but quiet. The threat is closer now — the seventh hour, with its Apophis confrontation, is the next event. The defenders have begun to prepare. Set's spear is no longer at rest. Mehen's coils are tightening again. Isis has begun to speak the protective words that will be needed at the seventh hour. Nephthys, whose function held the dissolution as sacred during the still center, is releasing that holding now — her work for the night's deepest hour is done, and the work of the next defender begins.

Practitioner Application

The sixth hour corresponds to the sleep that follows deep dreamless rest and precedes the dreaming of the later hours. Biological frameworks call this the gradual ascent through sleep stages — the body beginning the long process of returning toward waking, but not yet near waking. The cosmological frame names it differently: the *ba* is meeting the body. The reconstitution has begun.

You do not remember this hour, mostly. The sixth hour is not as fully suspended as the fifth, but it is closer to the still center than to the surface, and the conscious mind reaches it only in fragments if at all. Some practitioners have hypnagogic experiences that may correspond to this hour — the strange clear visions that arrive at the edge of waking but are not yet dreams of the kind that the later hours produce. Some have the sense of being assembled — of body and self coming back into alignment — which is the sixth hour briefly visible.

What most practitioners notice of the sixth hour is the gap-feeling at certain awakenings. The morning when the body is awake but the self has not yet fully returned to it. The minutes in which thought has not yet engaged and the body's sense of itself is the only presence. The orientation that has to occur before the day can begin — *where am I, what day is it, what am I doing today* — that you usually move through without naming. The gap is the sixth hour completing itself. The *ba* and the body are still in proximity rather than in union. The reconstitution has not yet finished.

This gap-feeling can carry texture. Mornings after particularly deep sleep often have a quality of tenderness in them — a softness in the body, a slowness in the mind, a sense of being newly arrived that the day has not yet covered over. This is the sixth hour's trace. The reconstitution is well underway by morning but not fully complete, and the first minutes of waking are sometimes experienced inside the reconstitution itself rather than after it.

There is also the morning that arrives carrying grief or sorrow that was not present the night before. This is not because grief was processed wrong or insufficiently. It is because the *ba* underwent a merging at the still center, and what was let go of in the merging was something the body did not yet know was being released. The sixth hour brings the *ba* back to the body carrying the alteration, and the body's first response to the altered *ba* can be grief — recognition that something is no longer being held that the body had been holding. This is reconstitution working correctly. The grief is the body acknowledging what the still center released.

The implication for daily practice is the threshold at dawn, which the original eight foundational chapters already established. The Dawn Rite is the practitioner's conscious meeting of what the sixth hour produced — the *ba* returning to the body, the reconstituted form arriving, the gap closing. The rite is performed within the seventh and eighth hours of the passage, when the *ba* and body have become re-fused enough that the practitioner can speak as one, but the rite acknowledges what the sixth hour did. The threshold at dawn is the inheritance of the deep waters.

The implication beyond daily practice is for the practitioner who has come through a longer fifth hour. If the still center has been a season of months or years rather than a few hours of one night, then the sixth hour is also longer. The reconstitution begins, but it begins slowly. The *ba* meets the body, but the body is not yet ready to be re-fused with what the *ba* has become. The practitioner who is in this stage of a longer passage may feel the gap-feeling not as the texture of a single morning but as the texture of a season — the sense that they are returning to themselves but have not yet fully arrived, that the reconstitution is occurring but is not finished, that something is different now and is still becoming what it will be.

This is correct. The sixth hour does not rush. It is the territory in which the meeting becomes the eventual reunion. The eventual reunion is the work of the remaining hours. What the sixth hour establishes is the proximity from which everything else proceeds.

In the **acknowledgment register**, the practitioner can recognize: *The dissolved aspect is meeting the body that waited. I am being reassembled. The reconstitution is beginning. I do not need to direct it.*

In the **devotional register**, the practitioner can offer: *Twelve gods of the deep, you witness the meeting. Ra, your ba meets your body. I am being put back together at a depth I cannot see. I acknowledge what is occurring.*

The hour itself asks only that you remain present in the cabin while the meeting at the heart of the deep waters proceeds.

A Guided Meditation for the Sixth Hour

This meditation is for use in the hours after the still center has been crossed — for the practitioner who wakes briefly in the deep-water

The cavern is behind you. The merging has occurred. You did not witness it.

(pause)

The barque has begun moving again. Not the smooth passage of the earlier hours — something slower, deeper. The water beneath the vessel is wider than the river that carried the barque before the still center. This is the territory of the deep waters.

(pause)

At the center of these waters, something is occurring that belongs to you in a particular way.

The *ba* — the aspect of you that descended into the burial mound at the fifth hour and merged with what waited there — is returning. It is altered. What it has been through is real and what it carries forward is real. It is moving now through the deep water toward something else.

What it is moving toward is the body. Your body, in the cosmological sense — the form that was left behind when the *ba* descended, the aspect that remained itself across the still center, the part of you that has been waiting.

(longer pause)

The two are about to meet.

You do not need to direct this. You do not need to understand what was changed in the *ba* or what the body has been holding while it waited. You only need to be present in the cabin while the meeting occurs at the heart of the deep waters.

(pause)

Notice that the meeting is not the same as the merging.

At the still center, the *ba* and Osiris's body became one. The dissolution was complete. Here, in the deep waters, the *ba* and your own body do not merge. They meet. They come into proximity. They remain themselves while being near each other for the first time since the descent.

This is reconstitution beginning. Not finished. Not yet the reunion at dawn that will allow you to wake as yourself. But begun.

(pause)

The twelve gods of the deep are present at the perimeter of the meeting. They do not act. They witness. The water holds the meeting. The barque passes slowly across the deep. The hour proceeds.

If you sense a texture in your body now — a softness, a tenderness, a sense of being newly arrived to yourself without quite knowing why — that is the sixth hour briefly visible. The *ba* has come close to the body. The body is registering the *ba*'s altered form. Something in you is being put back together at a depth your conscious mind cannot follow.

(longer pause)

If the morning brings unexpected grief, or unexpected clarity, or unexpected gentleness, these are the same hour's trace. The *ba* returned carrying what the still center let go of. The body received the altered *ba* and is responding to what is different. None of this is wrong. All of it is reconstitution at its beginning.

(pause)

Now release the meditation.

The hour continues without your attention. The *ba* and the body remain in proximity. The deep waters hold them. The crew attends. The defenders have begun their preparation for the seventh hour, but the seventh hour is not yet. The sixth hour is completing itself first.

What remains in you is only your weight, your breath, the dark behind your closed eyes — or the first light of morning, if the meditation has been used at the threshold of dawn rather than in the night.

Either is correct. The sixth hour reaches into both.

Rest now, if rest is what is asked.

Or wake, if waking is what is occurring.

The reconstitution is underway.

The Seventh Hour

The serpent waits. The defense holds. The passage continues.

What the Amduat Describes

The deep waters of the sixth hour end. The barque, slowed by their depth and quieted by the meeting at their center, enters a narrower channel. The walls of the corridor are stone. The river ahead, which has been wide and deep across the previous two hours, contracts into a passage scarcely wider than the Mesektet itself.

The territory of the seventh hour is the **cavern of Apophis.**

The serpent is waiting. He is depicted in the *Amduat* as enormous — large enough that his body coils across the entire width of the corridor, large enough that the barque cannot pass while he occupies the channel. His function is opposition. He does not attack out of malice or hunger. He is what stands against the passage at this hour, the way every hour has its inhabitants and every territory has its character. Apophis's character is opposition to the solar order, and the seventh hour is where that opposition is most fully present.

Around Apophis are twelve sandbars across the river. The serpent has been working since before the barque arrived — drying out the channel, beaching the path the Mesektet must travel, building the obstacle that will keep Ra from continuing the passage. If the sandbars hold, the barque cannot proceed. If the barque cannot proceed, the passage fails. If the passage fails, there is no dawn.

The defense begins before the barque reaches the corridor. Isis, whose magical work began intensifying at the end of Hour VI, is now speaking with full operative force at the stern. Her words are the structural maintenance that keeps the barque coherent under attack. Nephthys, who was at rest during the cavern, is now also speaking. The two sisters work in coordination — Isis maintains the barque's integrity, Nephthys binds the magical force of the attack against it.

Set takes his position at the prow. His spear has been ready since Hour VI's close. As the barque enters the corridor, Set strikes at the serpent. The spear engages the serpent's body. Each strike weakens the obstruction. The sandbars begin to fail. The water returns to the channel where it had been dried.

Selket, the scorpion goddess, appears in this hour. Her function is the binding. After Set's strikes have subdued Apophis sufficiently, Selket places the rope across the serpent's body and holds it. The serpent is restrained. He is not killed — Apophis cannot be killed, because what he represents cannot be eliminated from the cosmos. He is bound for the duration of this passage. Tomorrow he will be loose again. Tomorrow the same defense will be mobilized again. The recurrence is built into the system.

The Sons of Horus are present as ritual witnesses. The crew of the Mesektet — Hu, Sia, Heka, Wepwawet, the steersman — continues its functions, but those functions are coordinated with the defense rather than independent of it. Hu speaks the names that make the strikes effective. Sia perceives where the serpent is most vulnerable. Heka makes the binding magically operative. Wepwawet identifies the moment when the channel is clear enough for the barque to proceed.

When the channel clears — when the sandbars have been cleared by the water's return, when the serpent has been struck and bound, when the corridor is again navigable — the Mesektet passes. The serpent is behind. The eighth hour begins.

The Theological Claim

The seventh hour establishes the most uncomfortable claim of the entire Duat: **the night is contested, the contest is real, and the defense holds.**

The orientation chapter on the defenders said this in advance. The seventh hour is where it becomes operative. The reader has been carrying the knowledge of Apophis since the orientation; now the reader meets the hour in which Apophis is what is faced.

The discomfort of this claim is not the existence of opposition. Contemporary frameworks can accept that there are difficult nights, dreams that disturb, periods of sleep that feel like work. The discomfort is the *recurrence*. The barque tradition does not promise that opposition is occasional. It does not promise that the practitioner who has crossed difficult territory once will not cross it again. The seventh hour happens every night. The serpent is there every night. The defense is mobilized every night.

This is structural, not punitive. The eternal recurrence of Apophis is not a failure of the cosmology to defeat what should have been defeated. It is the cosmology's recognition that opposition to coherence is a permanent feature of reality. There is always a force in the universe that would unmake what has been made. The night does not banish this force. The night meets it, every cycle, and prevents it from succeeding.

What this means for the practitioner is that difficult nights are not anomalies. The night that brings a dream of dissolution, the night that surfaces something disturbing, the night that produces panic at 3 AM, the night that ends in a morning of disorientation — these are not signs that something has gone wrong with the practice or with the practitioner. They are signs that the seventh hour has been more visible than usual. The serpent is what it is. The defense is what it is. Both operate every night, and on some nights the practitioner notices.

The relief in this claim — and there is relief in it, properly understood — is the reliability of the defense. The practitioner is not asked to face Apophis. The practitioner has never been asked to face Apophis. The defenders are on the Mesektet. Set's spear engages. Isis speaks. Nephthys binds. Selket holds the rope. Mehen's coils maintain the protection of the cabin. None of this requires the practitioner's effort, awareness, or skill. The defense is constituted of intelligences whose function is precisely this hour, and they are present at this hour every night.

This is what the orientation chapter said in advance: *the defense holds.* The seventh hour is where the holding occurs. The chapter has been written so that the practitioner, on encountering a difficult night, has somewhere to locate the experience. The location is structural rather than personal. The seventh hour is what is happening. The defense has always already begun.

There is one further claim the seventh hour requires. Apophis cannot be defeated permanently because what Apophis represents — uncreation, dissolution-without-reconstitution, the force against coherence — is not a force that can be removed from the cosmos. It is part of what the cosmos contains. The Egyptian theology does not promise a future in which Apophis is gone. It promises a present in which Apophis is bound for the duration of each passage. This is what stability looks like in a cosmos that contains opposition: not the elimination of opposition, but the reliable, repeated, structural defense against it.

The practitioner is not promised a life without difficult nights. The practitioner is promised that the difficult night is always defended.

The Barque in This Hour

The Mesektet is most fully crewed in this hour. The crew that has functioned across the previous six hours is joined by the full force of the defenders, and additional ritual figures — the Sons of Horus, Selket, the binding goddesses — have appeared to perform their specific functions. The vessel is, in a sense, at maximum staffing for the seventh hour. This is what the entire night has been moving toward in terms of population: the moment when the most figures are present, doing the most coordinated work.

Ra remains in the cabin. He is at his most vulnerable here — more vulnerable than at the still center, even. At the cavern of Sokar, the threat was not active; the merging was the work, and the work proceeded without external opposition. At the seventh hour, the threat is actively engaged. Mehen's coils are at their absolute tightest around the cabin. The protection is operative because the protection is needed.

The practitioner who has been holding the orientation's claim about Ra's position — that the practitioner is analogous to Ra rather than to the crew — will feel the implication of that position most acutely in the seventh hour. You are in the cabin. The cabin is enclosed by Mehen. Outside the cabin, the defense is engaging the serpent. You cannot see the defense. You cannot know what is being done on your behalf. You can only be inside what is being defended.

This is the hour in which the practitioner's structural helplessness — the practitioner's inability to fight Apophis themselves — becomes most fully theological. You are not failing the night by not fighting. You are not abandoning the work by not engaging. The work is the defenders'. The cabin is yours. The relationship between these is the cosmology.

Set's spear is in active use. The sandbars are being cleared. The serpent is being struck. The structural maintenance of the passage is being performed by the figures whose function is precisely this. The barque is in the corridor of Apophis, and the corridor is the most dangerous territory of the entire night, and the danger is being met by what the night has prepared.

Practitioner Application

The seventh hour corresponds to several different experiences in the practitioner's life. They are united by a single character: they are the experiences in which the practitioner most directly encounters the contested nature of the night.

The most common is the dream that turns. The dream that begins as ordinary and then becomes threatening. The dream of being chased, of being attacked, of being trapped, of being unmade. The dream that produces panic and from which the practitioner wakes briefly before returning to sleep. This is the seventh hour briefly visible. Apophis is present in the territory. The defense is operating. The dream is the surface manifestation of the contest below it.

Less common but more disturbing is the 3-AM panic that does not have content. The waking that arrives carrying terror without object — no specific fear, no traceable thought, only the body's response to having been close to something the conscious mind cannot identify. This is the seventh hour reaching closer to awareness than usual. The defense is engaging something real, and the practitioner is briefly conscious adjacent to the engagement. The terror is not psychiatric; it is the body registering proximity to the contest.

Another form: the night that produces a morning of strange disorientation, where the practitioner feels they have been through something but cannot say what. This is the seventh hour completed without surface-level memory. Something occurred. The defense held. The practitioner crosses into the eighth and subsequent hours carrying the trace of having been close to Apophis without being able to name what was faced.

And the longer form, which most matters: the season in a practitioner's life when difficult nights repeat. The week or month or longer of sleep that does not feel restful, of dreams that disturb, of mornings that begin in disorientation. This is not failure of the practice or of the practitioner. This is the seventh hour being more visible than usual, across a season of nights. The serpent is more present in the practitioner's particular passage during this period. The defense is also more engaged. The crossing is being made every night, but the crossing is being noticed because the contest is closer to the surface than usual.

What the practitioner does with this knowledge is structural rather than active. You do not need to fight Apophis. You have never been asked to fight Apophis. The defense is constituted of figures whose function is the seventh hour, and they are present at the seventh hour of every night, and they are present at the seventh hour of every night during the longer seasons when the seventh hour repeats.

What you can do is rest more deliberately during such seasons. You can release the day at dusk with extra care, knowing that the night ahead will require more from the defenders. You can perform the Pre-Sleep Acknowledgment with full awareness that the cabin is what is being protected and that the protection is operative. You can wake, when you wake at 3 AM into territory you cannot name, and acknowledge: *I am in the seventh hour. The defense is engaging. I will return to the crossing.* You can stop interpreting the difficult night as failure.

There is one further thing the seventh hour offers, and it is for the practitioner who is in the longer form: the recurrence of the defense is also the reliability of the defense. If the night has been difficult for weeks, the defenders have engaged for weeks. They have not flagged. They have not abandoned the passage. They have not let Apophis through. The defense's reliability is what allows the practitioner to wake at all during such a season, because every night the corridor of the seventh hour has been navigated and the barque has passed.

You have not been alone in the difficulty. The cabin has been enclosed. The spear has been at the prow. The words have been spoken. The serpent has been bound, again, for this passage.

In the **acknowledgment register**, the practitioner can recognize: *The night is contested. The serpent is present. The defense is operative. I am in the cabin. The corridor is being cleared.*

In the **devotional register**, the practitioner can offer: *Set, your spear engages on my behalf. Isis, you speak the words I cannot speak. Nephthys, you bind what would unbind. Selket, you hold the rope. The defense holds. I acknowledge what is being done for me at this hour.*

The hour asks nothing more than presence in the cabin while the corridor is cleared.

A Guided Meditation for the Seventh Hour

This meditation is for use during a difficult night — for the practitioner who has woken in the deep hours carrying disturbance, or for the deliberate practice of meeting the seventh hour with framework rather than fear.

If you have woken into difficulty, settle first. The body that has been disturbed needs a moment to stop reacting. You do not need to resolve what woke you. You only need to be present here, in this meditation, while the body finds its way back to a position from which the meditation can be received.

(longer pause)

Take three slow breaths. Do not try to control them. Let them be ragged if they are ragged. Let them be uneven if they are uneven. The breath does not need to perform calm in order for the meditation to proceed.

(pause)

You are at the seventh hour.

The barque has entered a narrow corridor. The walls of the channel close in on both sides. Ahead, blocking the way, is the great serpent — Apophis, what stands against the passage at this hour every night. He has been working before the barque arrived to dry the channel and beach the path. The sandbars are across the river. The corridor cannot be passed while the serpent remains as he is.

(pause)

You are not being asked to face him.

This is the most important thing the seventh hour teaches, and it must land before the meditation can proceed. You are in the cabin. Mehen's coils are around the cabin at their tightest. You are inside what is being defended. Whatever has woken you, whatever disturbance has surfaced into the night, whatever fear or grief or dream-content has surfaced — you are not facing Apophis directly. The defenders are.

(pause)

Set has taken his position at the prow. His spear is engaging the serpent. Each strike clears the obstruction further. The sandbars are beginning to fail. The water is returning to the channel.

Isis is at the stern, speaking the words of structural maintenance. Her voice holds the barque coherent against the attack. Nephthys is also speaking, binding the magical force of the obstruction so that Set's strikes can be effective.

Selket has the rope. When Set has subdued the serpent sufficiently, Selket places the rope across his body and holds it. The serpent is bound for the duration of this passage. He cannot be killed. He will be loose again tomorrow. But for this night, he is restrained.

(longer pause)

This is what is happening below your awareness. This is what is happening regardless of whether you have woken into it. The defense is operating on your behalf, the way it operates every night, the way it has operated every night of your life.

If this is a difficult season — if difficult nights have been repeating — the defense has been operating for every one of them. None of those nights ended in the passage failing. None of those nights crossed without the serpent being bound. You woke each morning. You crossed each cabin. The defenders have not flagged.

(pause)

What is asked of you is what has been asked at every hour: remain in the cabin. Allow the defense to be the defenders'. Do not try to do what is not yours to do.

If terror is present in the body, let it be present without requiring it to leave. The terror is not the practitioner failing. The terror is the body registering proximity to the contest, and proximity is not the same as engagement. You are not engaged. You are in the cabin. The corridor will clear.

(longer pause)

The corridor is clearing now.

The serpent is bound. The sandbars are gone. The water has returned. The Mesektet is moving forward again through the channel. The seventh hour is completing itself. The eighth hour is ahead — the caverns of the assembled gods, the company that receives the barque after the great defense — but that is not yet. The seventh hour is finishing first.

(pause)

If you can return to sleep, return. The passage will continue without your conscious participation. The defenders remain at their stations. Mehen's coils remain tight around the cabin. You are still being defended even when you are unconscious within the defense.

If you cannot return to sleep, do not perform sleep. Stay where you are, awake within Nyx's household, carrying the knowledge of what is being done on your behalf. The morning will come. The eighth hour will move into the ninth and tenth and eleventh, and the dawn will arrive carrying what the night made.

You do not have to fight. You have never had to fight. The defense holds.

Rest now, if rest is what is asked.

The serpent is bound.

The Eighth Hour

You have come through. The chambers receive you. The company speaks.

What the Amduat Describes

The corridor of Apophis is behind. The serpent is bound. The sandbars are gone. The Mesektet passes out of the narrow channel of the seventh hour and into a region that opens into chambers — ten of them in the classical count, sometimes called the *qereret*, sometimes simply the caverns of the gods.

Each chamber contains a different group of divine beings. They are not the gods of the earlier hours — not the welcomers of Hour I, not the *bau* of the blessed in Wernes, not the organized dead of Hour III. The gods of the eighth hour have appeared specifically here, in this region after the great defense, and their function is reception.

The barque moves slowly through the chambers. The *Amduat* depicts the passage as deliberate — the vessel travels along a path that takes it past each chamber in sequence, and at each chamber the resident gods come forward to acknowledge Ra.

They speak. The text gives many of the speeches in full. The acknowledgments are formal and detailed, and they are not the same from chamber to chamber: each group of gods names a specific aspect of what the passage has accomplished and what remains to be done.

The substance of what is offered is specific. Strips of cloth — the linen used in wrapping the dead, here used to acknowledge the form that has come through dissolution. Vessels of water — the substance Apophis tried to dry from the corridor, now returned and offered. Ritual implements — the objects that confirm the passage's continuation in the language of ceremony. None of this is symbolic in the sense of representing something else. The cloth is cloth. The water is water. The implements are what they are. What is symbolic — what carries the theological weight — is the act of offering: the gods of each chamber confirming, by these gifts, that the barque has reached this point in the passage and that what comes next can proceed.

Ra is present in the cabin throughout. His diminished form has begun to alter. The *ba* that returned in the sixth hour and was preserved through the seventh is now being acknowledged in its altered state by the receiving gods. The acknowledgments are not addressed to the Ra-who-set; they are addressed to the Ra-who-has-been-through-the-merging-and-the-defense, the Ra who is becoming what he will be at dawn. The gods of the chambers know which Ra they are speaking to. Their speeches address that one.

The crew continues its functions but the work has changed quality again. Hu is speaking — a great deal of speech, in fact, because each chamber requires acknowledgment and Hu's voice is the barque's voice in these encounters. Sia perceives the character of each chamber and what it requires. Heka makes the offerings effective. Wepwawet has opened the way through the chamber-region. The steersman holds the slow course that allows the receptions to occur.

The defenders, for the first time since Hour VI, are at rest. Set's spear is set aside. Mehen's coils have relaxed, though they remain in place around the cabin. Isis and Nephthys have stopped speaking the protective words — the protection is no longer needed because the threat is past. The defense, in this hour, recovers from its own work.

When the barque has passed through all the chambers — when each group of gods has spoken and offered and been acknowledged in return — the vessel exits the chamber-region into the territory of the ninth hour. The eighth hour ends. The assembling continues.

The Theological Claim

The eighth hour establishes a claim that contemporary frameworks have almost no language for: **the territory after a difficulty is itself a territory, with its own gods and its own work.**

The dominant cultural account of difficulty is binary. Either you are in the difficulty or you are out of it. The crisis is occurring or the crisis has passed. The dream is disturbing or the dream is over. The grief is acute or it has resolved. The illness is in its hardest phase or you are recovering. The binary structure has no name for the territory in between — the hour that follows the worst without yet being arrival at the next thing.

The barque tradition names this territory. It is the eighth hour. The chambers of the assembled gods.

What occurs there is reception. Not resolution — the assembling of the renewed form is the work of Hours VIII through XI together, and the eighth hour completes only the first stage. Not return to ordinary — the practitioner is not back in the living hours, and will not be until the twelfth hour. What occurs is the formal acknowledgment, by figures present specifically for this purpose, that the passage has reached this point. The defense held. The corridor was cleared. The barque is continuing. The reception is the recognition of these facts.

The implication for the practitioner is structural. After the seventh hour — whether that hour is a single difficult night or a season of difficult nights — there is a stretch of territory before the practitioner has fully returned to the ordinary daily passage. This stretch has its own character. It is reception. The territory itself acknowledges what has been crossed, and the acknowledgment is part of how the reconstitution proceeds.

This applies to the night and to the longer arc. After a night that included the seventh hour's intensity — the dream that turned, the 3-AM panic, the disturbance that woke the practitioner into awareness of difficulty — the rest of the night, before dawn, is not simply "the rest of sleep." It is the eighth hour, the ninth, the tenth, the eleventh. Each has its work. The eighth hour's work is reception: the body and the mind being acknowledged, by structures the practitioner cannot see, as having come through.

This is the source of a phenomenon that contemporary frameworks struggle to explain: the strange peace that sometimes arrives in the hour or two before dawn after a hard night. The practitioner woke at 3 AM in difficulty, returned to sleep with disturbance, and then — sometime before the alarm — entered a stretch of unusually deep rest, from which they wake in the morning more refreshed than the night seemed to predict. The eighth hour produced this. The chambers received what came through. The reconstitution moved into the next stage. The peace was the reception's trace.

For the longer arc — the season of a life that has included an extended seventh hour — the eighth hour is the early period after the worst is structurally past. The grief that no longer occupies every waking moment. The illness that has begun to release its grip. The vocational crisis that has stopped escalating and entered the territory where what comes next can begin to be considered. This period is not return. The practitioner is not back to who they were. What is occurring is reception by figures the practitioner cannot see — structures of healing, of meaning-making, of biological repair, of communal acknowledgment — that confirm the passage has reached this point.

The eighth hour, in its longer form, is also the period in which the practitioner is most vulnerable to misreading what is occurring. Two errors are common. The first is impatience: treating the eighth hour as failed return, demanding that the consolidation be complete when it has only begun. The second is despair: treating the eighth hour as ongoing crisis, failing to recognize that the worst has actually passed and the work has shifted into a different register. Both errors come from the absence of a framework for the territory between crisis and resolution. The barque tradition provides the framework. The eighth hour is its own thing. It is not the seventh repeating, and it is not the twelfth arriving. It is the chambers, and the chambers do their own work.

What you do at the eighth hour is allow the reception. The gods of the chambers speak; you let them speak. The offerings are made; you allow them to be made. The acknowledgments are addressed to your altered form; you permit the addressing. None of this requires your active participation. The hour proceeds. What changes when you have the framework is that you stop trying to rush the consolidation or to interpret the slowness as failure. The barque moves slowly through the chambers because the chambers require slow movement. The eighth hour cannot be hurried.

The Barque in This Hour

The Mesektet has changed character again. It is no longer the laboring vessel of Rosetau, no longer the silent attendant of the cavern of Sokar, no longer the embattled barque of the seventh hour's corridor. It is a vessel being received. The water beneath it is calm. The chambers it passes are arranged to permit slow, deliberate transit. There is no urgency. The crew is active but unhurried.

Ra remains in the cabin, but the cabin is more open than it has been since the third hour. Mehen's coils have eased, though they have not unwound. The protection remains structurally in place, but its tension has reduced. Ra himself is more visible than he was in the deeper hours — his diminished form is no longer at its absolute reduction. Something of him is beginning to be assembled. The eighth hour is when that assembling begins to be visible from outside the cabin, even though it is not yet complete.

The crew's work is acknowledgment. Each chamber requires Hu to speak and be answered. The exchange between the barque and each receiving group of gods is the structural content of the hour. The exchanges are not perfunctory. The *Amduat* gives them at length because they are doing real work — the consolidation of what was dissolved depends on being recognized at each stage, and the recognition is exactly what the eighth hour provides.

The defenders, as noted, are at rest. This is the most important thing about the eighth-hour barque, structurally. Set's spear is set aside. Mehen has relaxed. Isis and Nephthys have stopped speaking the protective magic. The defenders are not absent — they remain on the vessel, ready for whatever the remaining hours might require — but their function is dormant. The eighth hour is not contested territory. The chambers of the assembled gods are not where opposition operates.

This rest of the defenders is what the practitioner sometimes feels as the strange peace before dawn. The internal defenders — the structures of vigilance that engage during the seventh hour's contests — are also at rest. The body's alarm systems have lowered. The mind's hyper-attention has eased. What remains is reception, slow movement, the acknowledgment of having come through.

Practitioner Application

The eighth hour corresponds to a specific stretch of sleep that contemporary frameworks rarely name. It is the period after the deep hours of the night have completed their hardest work and before the dreaming-toward-waking begins in earnest. In biological terms it is sometimes called the consolidation phase. In the cosmological frame it is the chambers of the assembled gods.

The practitioner experiences it, when they experience it, as the unusually deep rest in the hour or two before the alarm sounds. The sleep that feels different from the rest of the night — quieter, more whole, somehow more sufficient even though it is shorter in duration than the sleep before it. Not every night includes a noticeable eighth hour. Most nights it occurs without being felt. But the nights that have included real difficulty often produce a felt eighth hour — the body's recognition that the worst has passed and the reception has begun.

You do not need to do anything to receive the eighth hour. It occurs whether you witness it or not. What changes when you have the framework is that you stop suspecting it. The hour or two of unusually deep sleep before dawn, after a hard night, is sometimes treated by anxious practitioners as a problem — *did I oversleep, did I lose track of time, why was that sleep so different.* The cosmological frame names what occurred: the chambers received what came through. The reconstitution moved into its next stage. The unusually deep sleep was the reception's trace.

For the longer arc — the season of a life that has been through an extended seventh hour — the practitioner application is more important and harder to recognize. The eighth hour of a season is not a moment but a period. It can last weeks. It can last months. It is the territory in which the practitioner has stopped being in immediate crisis but has not yet fully returned. The temptation in this territory is to push past it, to insist on full return, to treat the slowness of the consolidation as evidence that something is still wrong. The barque tradition recommends, instead, the recognition that the eighth hour is itself a territory and has its own duration.

The chambers cannot be hurried. The gods of each chamber have specific acknowledgments to make and specific offerings to provide. If the practitioner moves too quickly through this territory — refuses the offerings, dismisses the acknowledgments, demands that the next hour begin before the current hour has completed — the consolidation suffers. The renewed form, when it finally assembles at the twelfth hour, will be less complete than it could have been.

This sometimes shows in practitioners who have come through a major life crisis but who returned to ordinary functioning too quickly. They are technically back in the living hours but something in them remains in the eighth hour, unconsolidated, the chambers' offerings ungathered. They look like they have returned. They are functional in the day. But the renewed form is not fully assembled. The eighth hour will continue to occur in them, in fragments, in the moments when the day-self quiets enough for the unfinished reception to surface.

What the eighth hour asks of the practitioner is the patience to allow reception. The chambers will speak. The offerings will be made. The acknowledgments will accumulate. None of this requires effort, but all of it requires the practitioner's continued presence in the territory rather than premature departure from it.

In the **acknowledgment register**, the practitioner can recognize: *I have come through. The chambers are receiving me. The reception is its own work. I do not need to rush.*

In the **devotional register**, the practitioner can offer: *Gods of the assembled company, you receive what has come through the corridor. You acknowledge the form that has been preserved. I accept what you offer. I remain in the chambers until the chambers have finished.*

The hour asks only that you stay long enough to be received.

A Guided Meditation for the Eighth Hour

For use in the hours before dawn after a difficult night, or as a deliberate practice on a day when the practitioner is in the longer territory after a season of difficulty. This meditation is quieter than the previous ones; the eighth hour itself is quiet, and the meditation should reflect that.

If you are reading this in the small hours, after waking from disturbance: notice first that the disturbance has eased.

(pause)

The corridor is behind. Whatever woke you, whatever surfaced into the night, whatever the seventh hour required of the defenders — it is past. The serpent is bound. The barque has passed through the channel.

You are now in different territory.

(pause)

The eighth hour is the chambers of the assembled gods. The barque has emerged from the narrow corridor into a region that opens out into rooms — ten of them, each containing a different group of divine beings, each with its own acknowledgment to offer.

The chambers do not threaten. They receive.

(pause)

You have come through. This is the first thing the gods of the chambers say. Not in those words — the *Amduat* gives their speeches at much greater length — but that is the substance. The barque is the barque that has come through the seventh hour. The Ra in the cabin is the Ra who survived the corridor. The crew is the crew that did the defense. The gods of the chambers acknowledge these facts. They name what has been preserved. They confirm what continues.

(longer pause)

Let yourself be received.

You do not need to do anything to receive what is being offered. The chambers offer cloth, water, ritual implements — substances that confirm the passage. The crew accepts each offering. Hu speaks the acknowledgments in return. The exchange is formal, unhurried, and necessary.

The reception is doing real work. The form that was dissolved at the fifth hour, met at the sixth, defended at the seventh — that form is now being acknowledged in its altered state by figures whose function is precisely this acknowledgment. Without the eighth hour's reception, the assembling of the renewed form could not continue. The chambers are not ornamental. They are structural.

(pause)

If you are in a longer eighth hour — if a season of your life has been in the territory after crisis but before full return — let this meditation address that season as well. The patience the eighth hour asks of the practitioner is not the same as enduring more difficulty. It is the patience of remaining in a territory whose work is slow.

You have stopped being in crisis. You have not yet fully returned. This is its own thing. This is the eighth hour. The chambers are still speaking. The offerings are still being made. The reconstitution is still consolidating. None of this is failure. All of it is exactly what is happening at this stage of the passage.

(longer pause)

Notice that the defenders are at rest.

Set's spear is set aside. Mehen has eased. Isis and Nephthys are no longer speaking the protective magic. The internal structures of vigilance — whatever in you was on alert during the seventh hour — those structures can also rest. The eighth hour does not require defense. The chambers are not contested.

This is the source of the peace that sometimes arrives in the hour before dawn after a hard night. The defenders have stood down. The vigilance has eased. The body that was tense is allowed to release. The mind that was hyperattentive is allowed to quiet. None of this is permanent — the defenders remain on the vessel and will engage again when needed — but for the duration of the chambers, they rest.

Let yourself rest with them.

(pause)

The barque continues slowly through the chamber-region. There is no hurry. The hour completes itself at the pace it requires. When the receptions are finished, the ninth hour begins — the offerings, the sustenance, the territory in which the reconstitution continues. But the ninth hour is not yet. The eighth is still doing its work.

(pause)

If you are returning to sleep, return. The reception will continue without your conscious attention. You will wake having been through the chambers, carrying what they offered, into the morning that is closer than the night now suggests.

If you are remaining awake, remain. The eighth hour can be inhabited consciously. The peace that has settled in the body is the reception's trace, available to you as recognition. You do not need to interpret it or hold it carefully. It is there because the chambers are doing their work.

Either is correct.

Rest now, if rest is what is asked.

The company is speaking.

The Ninth Hour

What was offered is returned. The crew is fed. The passage sustains itself.

What the Amduat Describes

The chambers of the assembled gods open onto a wider territory. The Mesektet, having moved slowly through the receptions of the eighth hour, enters a region the *Amduat* describes with unusual specificity. This is the hour of the **gods of the offering loaves, the gods of beer, the gods of bread** — twelve provision-deities whose function is to feed the crew of the barque.

The substance of the hour is distribution. The offerings made to the barque in the previous hour — the cloth, the water, the ritual implements, and other gifts whose names the *Amduat* lists at length — were not received passively. They were transformed by the receiving. Now, in the ninth hour, the gods of provision distribute the transformed substance to those who have been laboring on the vessel since the threshold.

Hu receives. Sia receives. Heka receives. Wepwawet receives. The steersman receives. The four defenders — Set, Mehen, Isis, Nephthys — receive. Each is fed by the gods whose function is precisely this feeding. The *Amduat* names specific provisions for specific figures: bread for those whose work requires the substance of sustained labor, beer for those whose work requires the loosening of the throat for speech, ritual loaves for those whose work is magical maintenance. The match between what is offered and who receives is not generic. It is calibrated.

The ninth hour also introduces the **sailors of Ra** — figures who have not been depicted as central in the earlier hours but whose function becomes visible here. The sailors row. The Mesektet, which has been variously carried by current, dragged by ropes, held stationary, and moved slowly through deep waters, is now being actively propelled. The sailors at the oars are part of the company being fed. They have been laboring as much as the crew, and they receive their portion alongside Hu and Sia and the others.

What is offered to Ra himself in this hour is more focused. Ra does not eat in the sense the crew eats — his diminished form does not require sustenance in the same way. What he receives is acknowledgment of his progression. The gods of provision speak directly to him. They name where the barque has come from and where it is going. They confirm that what was lost in the merging has been integrated, that what was preserved in the defense has been kept, that what was acknowledged in the chambers has been recorded into the structure of the passage. Ra receives this in silence. His altered form is now visible enough that the receiving gods address it directly.

The barque moves forward at the steady pace the sailors provide. The crew eats. The defenders eat. The sailors continue rowing. The ninth hour is in this respect the most ordinary-looking hour of the entire passage — the work of a vessel and its company being fed and moving forward — and that ordinariness is itself the theological point.

The Theological Claim

The ninth hour establishes a claim that contemporary frameworks have particular trouble with: **the passage is sustained by what the passage produces.**

What was carried into the night in Hour II — the day's content, the encounters and difficulties and unfinished thoughts — was distributed to the inhabitants of

Wernes as provision. The territory was fed by what the practitioner brought. What was acknowledged in the chambers of the eighth hour was the form that had come through dissolution, defense, and reception. The offerings made there were specific to that form. In the ninth hour, the offerings are returned — transformed by the receiving — to the crew that performs the labor of the passage. The substance that fed the territory in the early hours, after being changed by what the deeper hours did to it, now feeds the figures who propel the vessel forward.

The circle is closed. The passage is not sustained by something external to it. It is sustained by its own transformations of what it carries.

The passage is sustained by what the passage produces. The day's content becomes provision becomes labor becomes the propulsion that brings the barque to dawn. Nothing in the system is wasted. Nothing in the system arrives from outside. The cosmology is closed on itself, and the closing is what makes the passage reliable.

The implication for the practitioner is structural and beautiful. What you carried into the night was not residue to be cleared. It was provision to be transformed. The transformation has been occurring across the deeper hours, performed by the inhabitants of each region in their turn. By the ninth hour, what you brought has been changed into the substance that feeds the labor that carries you toward dawn. The grief that was given to the territory in Wernes is now part of what propels the sailors at their oars. The unfinished thought that was distributed in the second hour is now what permits Hu to speak the names of acknowledgment. The unprocessed encounter is now what allows Wepwawet to open the way forward.

You did not give the night nothing. You gave it what the day produced in you, and the night has been turning what you gave into what it requires to carry you forward.

This reframes the practitioner's relationship to the day's difficulty. The contemporary frame treats unresolved difficulty as a problem — something the practitioner should have addressed in the living hours and now has to "process" in sleep, often with the implication that the processing is incomplete or imperfect. The barque tradition reframes this: the unresolved is not a problem to be cleared. It is the raw material the passage requires. Without unresolved difficulty, there would be nothing for the deeper hours to transform. Without transformation, there would be nothing for the crew to be fed. Without feeding the crew, the passage could not continue.

The practitioner who arrives at sleep carrying difficulty is not failing. They are providing. The system depends on this providing.

For the longer arc, this claim becomes more important. The season of a life that has been through an extended fifth and sixth and seventh hour — the dissolution and the meeting and the defense, all extended across months rather than hours — has been generating provision the whole time. The practitioner who has been carrying grief or illness or vocational collapse has been feeding the structures that sustain the longer passage. By the season's ninth hour, what was carried has been transformed into the substance that allows the practitioner to continue. The friend who appears with the right thing at the right moment. The unexpected resource. The clarity that arrives without effort. These are the ninth hour visible in a longer arc: the system returning, through unexpected channels, what was given to it through the dissolution.

This is not divine reward for suffering. The barque tradition does not promise that grief produces gifts in proportion to its weight. What it promises is that the system is closed — that what was given to the territory by the practitioner is returned, transformed, through the channels that sustain the passage's continuation. Sometimes the return is small. Sometimes it is barely noticeable. Sometimes the practitioner is too tired to recognize it. The return occurs regardless. The ninth hour is structural.

The Barque in This Hour

The Mesektet is being actively rowed for the first time in the passage. The current that carried it through the earlier hours has resolved into a steadier propulsion: the sailors at the oars. The vessel moves at a pace that is neither the slow drift of Wernes nor the labored dragging of Rosetau nor the stationary attendance of the cavern of Sokar. It moves at the pace of work sustained by what has been received.

The crew is eating. Hu's voice, which has been working since the first hour, requires the loosening of throat that the offered beer provides. Sia's perception, which has been performing across regions of varying difficulty, requires the focused substance of the offering loaves. Heka's connective force, which has been making magic operative throughout the passage, requires what the gods of magical provision offer specifically to him. The eating is not symbolic. The eating is what permits the work to continue.

The defenders are also fed. This is what allows them to engage again, when engagement is required, in the remaining hours. The seventh hour drew on Set's ferocity, on Isis's spoken magic, on Nephthys's binding, on Mehen's coiled protection. The eighth hour rested the defenders. The ninth hour feeds them. By the time the tenth hour begins — which carries its own work, the regeneration of the wounded eye, with its own demands on specific figures — the defenders are restored and available.

The sailors have a particular role in this hour that they did not have before. They appear, in the *Amduat*'s depiction of the ninth hour, as if for the first time, though they have been present in the barque's structure throughout. Their function becomes visible because their function is exactly what this hour requires. The Mesektet must be propelled. The sailors propel it. They are fed alongside the crew because they are part of the crew, even if the earlier hours did not name them.

Ra remains in the cabin, but his form has continued to consolidate. The acknowledgments of the ninth hour are addressed to a Ra who is closer to dawn than the Ra of the previous hours has been. The diminishment that characterized him through the deepest hours has begun to ease. The form is not yet Khepri — that arrival belongs to the twelfth hour — but it is no longer the absolute reduction of the cavern of Sokar. The reconstitution that began in the sixth hour is accumulating substance.

Practitioner Application

The ninth hour corresponds to a stretch of late-night sleep in which dreams sometimes take on a particular character. Where the third hour's dreams were of the dead, where the seventh hour's dreams were of dissolution or threat, the ninth hour's dreams — when they occur — are often dreams of **provision**. Dreams of receiving food. Dreams of unexpected gifts. Dreams of being attended to. Dreams in which a need is met by something the dreamer had not asked for.

These dreams are easy to dismiss because they do not feel as significant as the dreams of difficulty. The dream in which a friend brings you exactly the meal you needed does not seem theologically weighty. The dream of being given something — a book, a key, a tool — does not feel like the deep work of the night. But these dreams are the ninth hour at the surface. The provision is occurring. The deeper structures are being fed. The dream is the visible trace.

The practitioner who has been carrying difficulty into sleep and who occasionally dreams of being fed or received or supported is seeing the system function. The ninth hour is doing its work, and the dream-record is briefly visible.

What this does not mean: the practitioner should not interpret these dreams as predictions of the day to come. The dream of being given a key is not a sign that something specific is about to be unlocked. The dream of unexpected meal is not a sign that an actual meal is coming. The dreams are not messages from the future. They are the surface of what is occurring beneath the surface in the same night — the ninth hour's distribution, briefly registering in the dream-record.

What it does mean: the night is taking care of itself. The system the practitioner consented to at dusk is feeding the figures whose labor brings the practitioner to dawn. The practitioner does not need to manage this. The practitioner does not need to participate in it. The practitioner consented to the crossing and is being carried, and the figures who do the carrying are being sustained by what the passage produces.

For the longer arc, the ninth hour shows in the seasons of a life through unexpected provision. The friend who reaches out at exactly the right moment. The book whose arrival cannot be explained by the practitioner's own seeking. The resource that appears just before it was needed. The clarity that arrives without effort, often in the morning, often after a difficult night, often carrying the recognition of what to do next.

These are not divine interventions in the way some traditions describe such moments. The barque tradition does not require belief that an external deity has selected this practitioner for a gift. What it offers is the structural account: the system you are inside is closed. What you gave to it through your difficulty has been transformed by the deeper structures and is being returned through the channels that sustain the passage. The friend who reaches out is part of the system. The book is part of the system. The clarity is part of the system. The system is feeding the figures who carry you forward, and you sometimes briefly see the feeding.

The practitioner who is in an extended ninth hour — a season of a life in which provision has begun to be visible after a long passage through difficulty — does not need to interpret each instance of provision as personal communication. What is occurring is structural. The system is doing what the system does. The practitioner can receive what is offered without needing to make it mean more than it means. The provision is returning. The crew is being fed. The barque is moving forward.

In the **acknowledgment register**, the practitioner can recognize: *The provision is being distributed. The crew is being fed. What I gave to the night is being returned through the figures that carry me. The system sustains itself.*

In the **devotional register**, the practitioner can offer: *Gods of provision, you feed the crew. Sailors of Ra, you row the vessel through the steady territory. I acknowledge what is being returned through your labor. I acknowledge that what I carried in is being transformed by what carries me forward.*

The hour asks only that the practitioner allow the provision to occur and, when occasionally it surfaces into the day, recognize it as part of the system rather than as anomaly.

A Guided Meditation for the Ninth Hour

This meditation is shorter than those of the previous hours because the ninth hour is structurally less dramatic than the hours that surround it. The hour does its work through ordinariness — the feeding of a working crew — and the meditation should reflect this. It is for use in the late hours of sleep, or as a deliberate practice when the practitioner wishes to acknowledge the system's sustenance.

The chambers are behind you. The receptions of the eighth hour have completed. The barque has moved into a wider, steadier territory.

(pause)

Notice that the vessel is being rowed.

The sailors of Ra have taken their positions at the oars. The Mesektet is being propelled now — not carried by current, not dragged, not held stationary, not drifting through deep waters, but actively moved forward by the labor of those whose work this is. The pace is steady. The rhythm is unbroken.

(pause)

The gods of the ninth hour are distributing provision to the crew.

Hu, who has been speaking since the threshold, receives what permits the voice to continue. Sia, who has been perceiving across regions of varying difficulty, receives what focuses perception for what remains. Heka, who has been making the connective force operative across all the transformations, receives what sustains that force. Wepwawet receives. The steersman receives. The defenders, who rested in the chambers, are being fed.

The sailors are being fed alongside them.

(pause)

What is being distributed is what the passage produced. The offerings made in the previous hour, transformed by the receiving, have become the substance that sustains the labor that carries you forward.

This means something specific that the night has been doing.

(longer pause)

What you carried into the night is what is now feeding the crew.

Not the difficulty itself — the difficulty was distributed long ago, in Wernes, in the second hour. What is feeding the crew now is what the deeper structures made of what you carried. The grief became something. The unresolved thought became something. The unprocessed encounter became something. The transformations have been occurring across the deeper hours, and now, in the ninth, the transformed substance is feeding the figures whose labor brings you to dawn.

You did not give the night nothing. The night required what you gave. The night has used what you gave to sustain its own continuation on your behalf.

(pause)

If a dream arrives in this hour — a dream of being fed, of being given something, of being attended to — let it be what it is. It is the ninth hour briefly visible. The system is feeding itself, and the feeding is registering in the dream-record. You do not need to interpret it. You do not need to anticipate that it predicts something in the day. You only need to recognize that the provision is occurring.

(pause)

If you are reading this in waking awareness — if the ninth hour of a longer season is the territory you are in — let the meditation address that season as well. The provision that has begun to appear in your days, the friend or the resource or the clarity that has arrived without your having sought it directly, is part of the system. What you carried through the longer dissolution and defense is being returned through the channels that sustain the longer passage. You do not need to question the provision. You only need to receive what is being offered.

(longer pause)

The barque continues forward at the pace the sailors provide. The crew eats. The defenders eat. The propulsion is sustained. The tenth hour is ahead — the regeneration of the wounded eye, the gathering of what has been preserved into the form that will arrive at dawn — but the ninth is still doing its work.

(pause)

What is asked of you here is what has been asked at every hour: nothing. The crew is fed without your intervention. The sailors row without your direction. The provision is distributed by the figures whose function this is. You remain in the cabin, being carried by labor that is being sustained by what you gave to the territory you have been crossing.

Rest now.

The crew is being fed.

The Tenth Hour

What was scattered is gathered. The form that will arrive at dawn is being assembled.

What the Amduat Describes

The territory of the ninth hour ends. The Mesektet, having moved steadily through the region of provision, enters the tenth hour and a different kind of water again. These are not the deep waters of Hour VI, where the *ba* met the body. These are wider, shallower, populated waters — and the population is specific.

The inhabitants of the tenth hour's water are figures in various stages of regeneration. The *Amduat* depicts them as bodies, some half-submerged, some afloat, some in postures of damage that is being repaired. They are the drowned, the wounded, those whose forms were damaged in earlier passages of the cosmological cycle, and they are here being made whole by specific gods whose function is restoration.

At the center of the tenth hour is the work of the **gathering of the eye**.

The eye — the *wedjat*, the Eye of Horus — was wounded in the conflict between Horus and Set, scattered in the violence of that conflict, and reassembled by Thoth into the form in which it now exists. This reassembly is not a single past event in Egyptian theology. It is an ongoing structural act, repeated at the tenth hour of every solar passage. The eye is gathered every night. The fragments are brought back. The wholeness is reconstituted.

A note before this hour proceeds. The Eye of Horus has been absorbed into a great deal of contemporary material that has nothing to do with Egyptian theology — third-eye iconography, conspiracy symbology, generic sacred-geometry design language, jewelry for sale at New Age conferences. The chapter has to set this aside before the actual Egyptian theology can be received. The wedjat eye is not a symbol of mystical sight. It is the gathered form of what was scattered by violence. It is a record of damage and a record of repair. The amulet that depicted it — the most common protective amulet in Egyptian material culture — was carried because it asserted, in compact form, that wholeness can be reconstituted from fragments. That is what the tenth hour does, and what the eye on the amulet shows.

The work of the gathering is performed by a specific company. Thoth is the central figure — the god of writing, calculation, and structural restoration — whose function is to know which fragment belongs where. He is attended by other gods specific to this hour, sometimes called the eye-gathering gods, whose function is to bring each piece from where it has been kept and place it in the eye's structure. The pieces have been distributed across the entire passage. Each hour has held one or more of them. The tenth hour is when they are returned and reassembled.

What is being gathered is not only the eye. The eye is the structural image, but the gathering applies to more than the eye itself. The renewed form of Ra that will arrive at dawn as Khepri is also being assembled here. The merging at the still center produced an altered *ba*. The meeting at the sixth hour brought the *ba* back to the body. The seventh hour defended both. The eighth hour received the form and acknowledged it. The ninth hour fed the workers. The tenth hour is where the actual reassembly of the renewed Ra occurs — piece by piece, gathered from where each piece has been kept, placed back into the structure that will be the dawn-form.

The barque moves slowly through this region. The crew is present at the gathering but does not perform it; the gathering belongs to Thoth and the eye-gathering gods. The pace is deliberate. The work cannot be hurried. Each fragment requires its specific placement, and the placement requires that Thoth knows which fragment belongs where.

When the gathering is complete — when the eye has been reassembled and the renewed form of Ra is structurally present in the cabin — the tenth hour ends. The eleventh hour begins. The form that has been gathered now must be prepared for emergence.

The Theological Claim

The tenth hour establishes a claim that resolves something the practitioner has been carrying without name since the fifth hour: **the wholeness that arrives at dawn is the gathered form of what was scattered, not the unscattered original.**

The fifth hour took the practitioner apart. The dissolution was real. What occurred at the still center was the merging of the *ba* with what waited for it in Osiris's tomb, and what returned from that merging was altered. The body that received the altered *ba* in the sixth hour was, structurally, the same body — but the body's relationship to what now inhabited it had to be reconstituted. The reconstitution has been occurring across Hours VI, VII, VIII, and IX. The tenth hour is where the reconstitution becomes a **specific assembled form** rather than a process underway.

That assembled form is not the return of who the practitioner was at dusk.

This is the theological claim the chapter has to hold without softening: the practitioner who arrives at dawn is not the practitioner who fell asleep. The renewed form is the gathered form. It carries the marks of what scattered it. The eye that was wounded and reassembled by Thoth is still, structurally, the wounded eye — it is not made un-wounded by being gathered; it is made *whole as gathered*, which is a different state.

Wholeness, in the Egyptian theological sense, is not the original undamaged state. Wholeness is the gathered fragments held in a form that demonstrates that gathering is possible. This is a different claim than the contemporary frameworks that treat healing as restoration-to-prior-condition. The barque tradition does not promise that the practitioner who lost something at the still center will receive it back unchanged at dawn. What it promises is that what was lost will be gathered, and the gathering will be assembled into a wholeness that can carry the practitioner into the living hours.

The implication for the practitioner is structural and difficult. You will wake as a gathered form. The wholeness you arrive in at dawn is real — but it is the wholeness of the assembled, not the wholeness of the never-broken. The grief of yesterday has not been erased. The unfinished thought has not been resolved into resolution. The unprocessed encounter has not become processed in the sense that contemporary frameworks suggest. What has occurred is the gathering — the fragments have been brought back to their structural positions, and the form that holds them is reassembled.

This is what wholeness actually is. It is not absence of damage. It is the presence of all the parts in a form that holds them together.

The longer-arc implication is more important and more demanding. The season of a life that has been through dissolution, defense, reception, and provision is now, at its tenth hour, in the territory of the gathered form. The practitioner who has been through grief or illness or vocational collapse does not return to who they were before. The return is to a self that is gathered — a self whose components include what was scattered by the difficulty, now reassembled, marked by what scattered them. The grief is in the form. The illness is in the form. The collapse and what it taught is in the form. These are not residues to be cleared. They are structural pieces of the wholeness that arrives.

This is what the practitioner who has come through a major life passage sometimes recognizes in the morning when they look in a mirror or pause in a moment of unexpected stillness: *I am not who I was, and I am whole.* The two claims are not in contradiction. The wholeness is the gathered form. The form bears the marks of what scattered it. The wholeness is real.

The contemporary frameworks that promise erasure-of-damage as the criterion of healing are offering something the barque tradition does not offer. They are also offering something that does not occur in the passage. The eye does not return to its un-wounded state; the eye is gathered. The form that arrives at dawn is the gathered form. This is what is given. What is given is sufficient.

The Barque in This Hour

The Mesektet moves slowly through the regenerating waters. The crew attends to the gathering rather than performing it. Hu speaks the names of the fragments as they are brought — each piece of the eye has its own name, each component of the renewed form has its own designation — but Hu's voice in this hour is quieter than in the chambers of the eighth or the provision of the ninth. The naming serves the gathering rather than directing it.

Sia perceives the entire structure of what is being assembled. He sees, in the way Sia sees, the relationship between each fragment and the position it must occupy. He does not announce this. The eye-gathering gods know their work. Sia's perception is for the barque's record, not for the work itself.

Heka makes the assembly operative. Each piece, as it is placed, must become functionally part of the form. Heka's connective force is what produces this functioning. Without Heka, the gathering would be inert — pieces arranged in their correct positions but without animation. With Heka, the pieces become a living structure.

Wepwawet has opened the way through the regeneration waters and is now stationed at the bow of the barque, ready for the work of the eleventh hour. His preparatory function for the gates that will open at the eleventh has already begun.

The defenders are present but inactive. The eye-gathering is not contested territory. Set's spear remains at rest. Mehen's coils have eased further. Isis and Nephthys observe but do not work magic here. The gathering belongs to Thoth.

Ra in the cabin is in the most consolidated form he has held since the fourth hour, before the descent into Sokar's cavern. The *ba* and the body are integrated. The form that the gods of the eighth hour acknowledged has been assembled across the ninth and tenth hours. What remains is preparation for the emergence, which is the work of the eleventh.

Practitioner Application

The tenth hour corresponds to a late-night stretch of sleep in which the dreams shift character again. Where the ninth hour's dreams were often of provision, the tenth hour's dreams — when they occur — are often of **gathering**. Dreams of finding lost objects. Dreams of pieces coming together. Dreams of completing something whose components had been scattered. Dreams in which the dreamer is given the missing piece of something they had been holding incomplete.

These dreams have a different texture from the dreams of receiving. The dream of being fed is a dream of needs being met. The dream of gathering is a dream of pieces being reassembled. The practitioner who dreams of finding a key that fits an old lock, or of completing a puzzle, or of locating something that had been lost —

these are the tenth hour briefly visible. The form for the coming day is being assembled in the deeper structure, and the dream-record carries fragments of the assembly into the surface.

You do not need to remember these dreams for the gathering to occur. The work happens whether or not the dream-record is preserved. What changes when the framework is available is that the practitioner who does remember such a dream has a structural location for what occurred. The dream of pieces coming together is not random brain activity. It is the surface of Hour X.

For the longer arc, the tenth hour shows in the season of a life when the practitioner begins to recognize that what they were is being assembled into what they are becoming, and that the becoming includes the damage. This is the moment of looking in the mirror — perhaps months or years after a major life passage — and seeing a face that is not the face of the person who entered the passage and not the face of the person who would have existed without the passage. The face is the gathered face. The damage is in the form. The form is whole.

This recognition is often quiet. It is not the dramatic moment of healing that contemporary frameworks promise. The practitioner who has come through a long passage does not usually have a moment of revelation in which everything resolves. What they have, instead, is the gradual recognition — sometimes occurring across many small moments — that the gathering has occurred. The grief is in them. The grief is part of the form. The form is whole.

This recognition has its own quality of relief that is different from the relief of resolution. Resolution would mean the difficulty had been removed. Gathering means the difficulty has been incorporated into a form that holds it without being destroyed by it. The relief of gathering is the relief of carrying what cannot be released, in a form that can carry it. This is the wholeness the tenth hour produces.

The practitioner who is in the longer tenth hour can sometimes participate consciously in the gathering by attending to what the season's difficulty has produced in them that they would not otherwise have. The capacities that were forged in the difficulty. The understandings that the difficulty made available. The relationships that the difficulty either revealed or destroyed, leaving in either case a clarity about what was real. These are not silver linings. They are not the difficulty being justified. They are the components of the gathered form — the pieces that the difficulty made and that are now part of the wholeness that holds the practitioner.

In the **acknowledgment register**, the practitioner can recognize: *I am being gathered. What was scattered across the passage is being reassembled. The form that arrives at dawn will be the gathered form. The gathering is wholeness.*

In the **devotional register**, the practitioner can offer: *Thoth, you gather what was scattered. Eye-gathering gods, you bring back what was kept across the passage. I acknowledge what is being assembled in me. I accept the form that the gathering produces.*

The hour asks only that the practitioner allow the assembly to proceed and, when they recognize the gathered form in themselves, not insist on the un-scattered original.

A Guided Meditation for the Tenth Hour

For use in the late hours of sleep before the eleventh hour begins, or as a deliberate practice for the practitioner who is in the longer arc of a life-passage and is beginning to recognize the gathered form in themselves.

The ninth hour is behind you. The crew has been fed. The barque is being rowed steadily forward.

(pause)

The territory has changed again. The water beneath the vessel is wider here and shallower than before. There are figures in the water — bodies being restored by gods specific to this hour, forms being regenerated by the work that the tenth hour performs.

You are in the territory of the gathering.

(pause)

At the center of this hour is the work Thoth performs.

The Eye of Horus was wounded in the conflict between Horus and Set.
The wound scattered the eye into fragments. Thoth gathers the fragments.
He knows where each piece has been kept across the passage. He brings

them back from the hours that held them. He places each fragment into its structural position.

This work is occurring now.

(longer pause)

The eye is the image. The gathering applies to more than the eye.

What was dissolved at the still center has been moving toward this hour. The fragments of you that were scattered in the merging have been kept across the deeper hours — each hour holding what belonged to it. Now Thoth and his attendants are bringing each piece back and placing it in its position. The form that will arrive at dawn is being assembled.

This is not restoration to who you were yesterday. This is not the return of the un-scattered original. The gathering produces a different state.

(pause)

The wholeness that is being assembled in you is the gathered wholeness.

Let this land before the meditation continues. The form that will arrive at dawn is the form gathered from fragments. It bears the marks of what scattered it. The grief is in the form. The unresolved is in the form. What occurred in the deeper hours has not been erased — it has been incorporated into the structure of what is being assembled. The wholeness includes the marks of damage. The wholeness is what holds the marks to-gether.

(longer pause)

If you have been through a long passage — a season of a life that has included real dissolution, real defense, real grief or illness or collapse — let the recognition of the gathered form land for that season as well.

You are not who you were before the passage. You will not become who you were before the passage. What is occurring is not restoration to a prior state. What is occurring is the assembly of a form that includes what the passage scattered and what the passage produced in you. This is wholeness. The wholeness is real. The wholeness bears the marks.

This is the relief the tenth hour offers — relief that does not require the difficulty to be erased. The difficulty has been gathered into the form. The form can carry it. The form is whole.

(pause)

Notice that Thoth does not work alone.

The eye-gathering gods attend. They bring each fragment from where it has been kept across the passage. They place each piece into the structure. The work is precise. The work is deliberate. The work is not hurried, because the placement of each fragment requires that the fragment be placed exactly where it belongs.

In the deeper structure of you, the same work is occurring. What was scattered is being returned to its position. The position is not always the position the piece occupied before the scattering — sometimes the gathering produces a configuration that did not exist before. The wholeness is the gathered wholeness. The form is the form the gathering produces.

(longer pause)

If a dream arrives in this hour — a dream of finding something lost, of completing something incomplete, of pieces coming together — let it be what it is. It is the tenth hour briefly visible in the dream-record. The gathering is occurring. The dream is the surface of the assembly.

If you are reading this in waking awareness, in the longer season's territory: let the meditation address that season. The face you see when you catch yourself in an unguarded moment in the mirror — the face that is not who you were and is not the imagined-other-self that the passage might have produced — that face is the gathered face. The recognition that you are different and that you are still yourself is the tenth hour completing itself in a slower form.

(pause)

What is asked of you here is the willingness to receive the gathered form.

Not to mourn the unscattered original. Not to insist that the wholeness must be the wholeness of the never-broken. The barque tradition does not offer that. What it offers is the gathered wholeness, which is what is being assembled, and which is real.

You will wake into the form that is being made.

(pause)

The barque continues slowly forward through the regenerating waters. The eye is being gathered. The renewed form is being assembled. The eleventh hour is ahead — the preparation for emergence, the gates that begin to open — but the tenth is still doing its work.

What remains in you is only your weight, your breath, the dark behind your closed eyes, and the recognition that something is being put together in you that was scattered earlier in the passage.

Rest now.

The form is being assembled.

The Eleventh Hour

The territory is ordered for the dawn. The gates open in sequence. The farewell begins.

What the Amduat Describes

The regenerating waters of the tenth hour give way to a different territory. The Mesektet, carrying the gathered form, enters the eleventh hour and a region whose character is one of preparation. The water narrows again — not into the threatening corridor of the seventh hour, but into a channel that focuses the vessel toward what is ahead.

The territory of the eleventh hour is the **preparation for emergence**.

At the center of the hour is a serpent. This is not Apophis — Apophis was bound at Hour VII and remains bound through the rest of the passage. This is a different serpent, called in some recensions *Mehen-she*, sometimes simply *the coiled one of the horizon*. The serpent's body is the structural form through which Ra's renewed form must pass in the final shaping before dawn.

The function of this serpent is not protection in the way Mehen protected the cabin in the deeper hours. The function is shaping. The renewed form enters the serpent's body and moves through its length, and the movement completes the assembly that began at the sixth hour and continued across Hours VII through X. By the time the form emerges from the serpent at the other end, it is structurally ready for the eastern horizon. The shaping cannot be skipped. The dawn requires a form that has been through this final passage.

Beyond the serpent are the **gates of the horizon**. The *Amduat* depicts these as a sequence — sometimes seven, sometimes twelve, depending on the recension — through which the barque must pass before it can reach the position from which the dawn-crossing is possible. Each gate has its attendant gods. Each must be opened in sequence; none can be skipped, none can be opened out of order. The gods who open each gate speak specific words that the next gate's attendants are listening for. The structure is precise.

A specific work of this hour is the **disposal of the enemies of Ra**. Across the entire night the barque has encountered obstacles — the serpents of Rosetau driven back by Set's spear in the fourth hour, the lesser opponents at various gates, demons of the regions the passage crossed. None of these were killed. They were defeated and left behind in their respective territories. In the eleventh hour, the gods of this region collect them and place them into specific containment structures — pits, ovens, sealed chambers — where they will remain through the daylight hours and from which they will emerge to be defeated again on subsequent nights.

This is not punishment of the defeated. It is sorting. The territory must be cleaned of the night's obstacles before the new day can begin. The pits and ovens are administrative structures, not theological ones. The cosmos requires that opposition be contained where it can be re-engaged in the next cycle, and the eleventh hour performs that containment.

There is one further work of the eleventh hour, and it is the most quietly important: the **arousing of the dead**.

The gods of the eleventh hour speak to the inhabitants of the regions the barque has passed through. The dead of the third hour are addressed. The *bau* of Wernes are addressed. The gods of the chambers from the eighth hour are addressed. The figures fed in the ninth hour are addressed. The regenerating bodies of the tenth hour are addressed. The address is the same in substance: *the barque is leaving. The dawn approaches. The cycle is completing. The Duat itself will rest until the Mesektet returns at the next dusk.*

This is farewell. Not departure in the personal sense — Ra is not saying goodbye to specific inhabitants — but the structural notice that the passage is concluding and the territory is being released from the activity of the crossing. The inhabitants resume their permanent functions. The barque finishes its work. The boundaries that the passage maintained will dissolve briefly into the territory's resting state before the next dusk recreates them.

The barque moves through the gates as they open. The renewed form passes through the shaping serpent. The defeated are sorted. The dead are aroused to the knowledge that the cycle completes. The eleventh hour proceeds.

When the final gate opens — the gate that gives onto the eastern horizon — the eleventh hour ends. The twelfth hour begins. The dawn-crossing is at hand.

The Theological Claim

The eleventh hour establishes a claim that resolves something the practitioner has been carrying since the threshold at dusk: **the territory the passage crosses must be ordered before the new day can begin, and the ordering includes farewell.**

The claim has two parts. The ordering is the easier part. The territory the barque crossed contains the defeated, the regenerating, the assembled, the gathered, and all of these must be returned to their resting positions before the dawn. The pits and ovens for the defeated. The completion of the assembly for the renewed form. The opening of the gates in sequence. None of this is dramatic. All of it is necessary. The dawn cannot occur in a territory that has not been ordered.

The farewell is the harder part.

The eleventh hour is the structural location of the recognition that the passage is ending. Not the practitioner's passage through life — the cosmology does not address that — but this particular night's passage through the Duat. The barque is leaving the territories it crossed. The crew that performed the labor is preparing to release the night's specific work. The inhabitants of each region are being told that the activity of the crossing is completing, and that they will return to their permanent functions in the territory once the Mesektet has passed beyond the eastern gate.

This farewell matters for the practitioner because it carries something the contemporary frameworks do not name: **the night that worked on you is itself ending, and the ending has its own quality of grief.**

This is the strange melancholy that arrives sometimes in the very last hour of sleep before waking. The sense — sometimes barely conscious, sometimes vivid — that something is concluding. The body is not yet awake, but the night is no longer fully holding the body. The work of the deeper hours has been completed. The form has been gathered. The territory is being ordered. The dawn is structurally imminent. And in this stretch, the practitioner sometimes feels — without knowing why — a quiet grief, a sense of leaving a place where work was done, a recognition that the territory the night carried them through is closing behind them.

This is the eleventh hour briefly visible. The farewell to the territories the practitioner has been crossing is registering at the surface.

The practitioner who experiences this melancholy and treats it as a problem — *why am I sad in the morning, what is wrong* — is misreading the structural occurrence. Nothing is wrong. The night is closing. The territory that was crossed is being released. The barque is leaving regions that carried specific work, and the leaving has its own register. The practitioner is briefly aware of the leaving. The awareness is grief because all leaving is grief in some structural sense, even the leaving of a territory the practitioner could not consciously witness.

The relief here is the same as in earlier hours: this is not the practitioner's failure. This is the eleventh hour completing its farewell work, and the farewell is structural rather than personal. By the time the dawn arrives, the farewell will have been completed and the practitioner will cross the threshold into the living hours carrying the night's product without the night's territories. The territories will not be available again until the next dusk reopens them.

For the longer arc — the season of a life that has been through dissolution, defense, reception, provision, and gathering — the eleventh hour shows in the territory just before the return to ordinary life. The practitioner who has been through a major life passage and who is now structurally ready to resume the daily passage in their new form sometimes experiences a quiet grief in this final preparatory stretch. The grief is not regret for the passage. It is the farewell to the territory the passage occupied — the specific seasons of dissolution and gathering that will not be returned to in the same form. The practitioner is leaving regions of their own life that carried specific work, and the leaving has its quality of melancholy.

This is also structural. The next dusk of a life will open different territories. The seasons that are ending are ending. The practitioner who feels this is not failing to be grateful for the gathered form. They are completing the eleventh hour of a longer arc, and the eleventh hour is when farewell is performed.

One more thing the eleventh hour establishes, and it is the most quietly important. The gates open in sequence and cannot be skipped. The renewed form must pass through the shaping serpent and cannot bypass the shaping. The defeated must be sorted before the dawn. The dead must be aroused to the cycle's completion. None of this can be hurried.

The eleventh hour cannot be skipped. The temptation in any preparation is to leap to the arrival — to skip the final stretch and go directly to what is at the end. The cosmology does not permit this. The dawn requires the eleventh hour. The gates require their sequence. The shaping requires the serpent's body. The territory requires the farewell. What is being assembled and sorted and addressed in the eleventh hour is what permits the twelfth hour to occur as it occurs. Skip the eleventh and the twelfth cannot be the twelfth.

This applies to the practitioner. The morning that is rushed past — eyes opened, phone reached for, day begun without acknowledgment of the territory just left — is a morning in which the eleventh hour's farewell did not have its full duration. The practitioner crosses into the living hours carrying the night's product, but the territories that produced the product were not properly released. Over time, this builds up — a practitioner who skips the eleventh hour reliably arrives at increasing fatigue, increasing sense of disconnection from the night's work, increasing inability to remember what the deeper hours did for them.

The Dawn Rite that the original foundational chapters established — the threshold practice for the morning — is, in part, the practitioner's conscious participation in the eleventh hour's farewell. The rite is performed at the threshold of the twelfth hour, but it acknowledges what the eleventh has just completed. The territories have been released. The form has been gathered. The dawn is arriving. The Dawn Rite is the practitioner's recognition of this, and it carries the eleventh hour's farewell into conscious form.

The Barque in This Hour

The Mesektet moves through the gates of the horizon. The pace is steady. The crew is active but unhurried. The work of the eleventh hour is precise, sequential, and not subject to acceleration. Each gate opens in its own time. The next gate cannot be approached until the current one has been fully opened. The barque waits at each threshold for the work to complete.

The crew is more vocal in this hour than at any point since the chambers of the eighth. Hu speaks the words required to address each gate. The names of the gate-attendants must be spoken correctly for the gate to open. The names of the inhabitants being aroused — the dead, the *bau*, the chamber-gods, the regenerating bodies — must be spoken so that the farewell is registered. Hu's voice is doing structural work in this hour, and the work is sustained from gate to gate.

Sia perceives the configuration of each gate and the order in which the words must be spoken. The eye-gathering that Thoth performed in the tenth hour has produced a fully assembled perception in Sia — he is at his most acute in this hour, because the eleventh hour requires the maximum precision of perceptual work. Heka makes the words operative; each utterance, made functional by Heka's connective force, opens what it addresses.

Wepwawet has been at the prow since the close of the tenth hour. The opening of the way that has been his function across the entire passage culminates here. Each gate is opened by the gate-attendants, but Wepwawet is the figure who has identified the sequence, who knows which gate comes next, who has been preparing the barque for this final stretch. His work approaches its completion.

The defenders remain present but inactive. The eleventh hour is not contested territory. Set, Mehen, Isis, and Nephthys observe the gate-openings and the farewells but do not engage. Their work has been completed in the earlier hours. They are at rest in the cabin's vicinity, accompanying the renewed form toward dawn.

Ra in the cabin is now structurally close to Khepri without yet being Khepri. The shaping through the eleventh hour's serpent is completing the final preparation of the dawn-form. The Ra who passes through the gates is recognizable as the god who will emerge at the eastern horizon, but he is not yet that god. The transformation completes at the twelfth hour's threshold; the eleventh prepares the form for the completion.

Practitioner Application

The eleventh hour corresponds to the final stretch of sleep before waking — the territory in which the body is preparing to wake but has not yet woken, in which the mind is beginning to assemble its waking-form but is not yet in waking awareness.

Biological frameworks call this the transition from REM into the brief pre-waking interval. The cosmological frame names it differently: the gates are opening, the form is being shaped, the territory is being ordered, the farewell is being performed.

You may sometimes briefly inhabit this hour consciously — the half-waking, where you are aware that you are about to wake but have not yet crossed into full waking. The body is heavy. The mind is slow but functioning. There is sometimes a quality of recognition — *I am about to wake* — that is itself a registration of the eleventh hour. The form is being prepared. The dawn is structurally imminent. The practitioner is briefly aware of the preparation.

The melancholy that sometimes arrives in this stretch is the farewell registering. The practitioner who notices a quiet sadness in the very last sleep before waking — a sadness without object, a grief without content — is experiencing the eleventh hour's farewell at the surface. The territories that the night crossed are being released. The barque is leaving regions where work was done. The leaving has its quality, and the quality is registering.

This melancholy does not require interpretation. It does not need to be tracked back to a specific source or processed for meaning. It is the structural occurrence of the eleventh hour. Acknowledging it is sufficient. *The night is closing. Something is being left behind. I am preparing to emerge.*

For the longer arc, the eleventh hour shows in the period before the practitioner returns to the daily passage after a major life passage. The week or month before resuming ordinary work after a long illness. The stretch before the new vocational direction becomes operative. The time when the gathered form is in place and the return to the living hours is imminent but has not yet occurred. This stretch has its own grief — the farewell to the territories of the passage, which will not be returned to in the same form.

The practitioner in this longer eleventh hour does well to allow the farewell its duration. The temptation is to rush back to ordinary life as soon as the gathering is complete. The cosmology recommends, instead, the deliberate inhabitation of the preparatory stretch. The gates open in sequence. The shaping serpent must be passed through. The defeated must be sorted. The dead must be told the cycle is completing. None of this can be skipped, and the longer eleventh hour's farewell is performed in the practitioner who allows the preparatory stretch its full work.

What this looks like, practically: the practitioner who has come through a major passage and who is now structurally ready to resume the daily life sometimes does best by giving themselves a specific period of acknowledged preparation. Not avoidance of return — the return is what is preparing — but the conscious recognition that the eleventh hour requires its time. The week of quiet before resuming the demanding work. The month of slower pace before the new vocational direction is engaged. The stretch of acknowledged preparation in which the farewell to the longer passage's territories is allowed to occur.

The practitioner who does this is doing what the eleventh hour does. The gates are being opened in sequence. The form is being shaped through its final preparation. The territories are being released. The farewell is being performed.

In the **acknowledgment register**, the practitioner can recognize: *The territory is being ordered. The gates are opening. The farewell to what carried me is being performed. I am being prepared for the dawn.*

In the **devotional register**, the practitioner can offer: *Gods of the eleventh hour, you open the gates in sequence. Coiled one of the horizon, your body shapes the renewed form. Companions of the night that carried me, I acknowledge your farewell. I prepare to emerge.*

The hour asks the practitioner to allow the preparation its duration and not skip the farewell.

A Guided Meditation for the Eleventh Hour

For use in the very late sleep before waking, or as a deliberate practice for the practitioner in the longer arc of a life-passage who is preparing to return to the daily passage in their gathered form.

The tenth hour is behind you. The form has been gathered. What was scattered has been assembled.

(pause)

The barque has entered a different territory. The water has narrowed. The pace has steadied. The gates of the horizon are visible ahead.

You are at the eleventh hour. The preparation for emergence.

(pause)

At the center of this hour is a serpent. Not Apophis — Apophis was bound at the seventh hour and remains bound. This serpent serves the passage. The coiled one of the horizon. The shaping serpent.

The renewed form passes through the serpent's body. The movement completes the final preparation. The form that emerges at the other end is structurally ready for the eastern horizon.

You are passing through the shaping now.

(longer pause)

Beyond the serpent are the gates. Seven gates, twelve gates, depending on the recension — but each must open in sequence. None can be skipped. The gods of each gate speak the words that the next gate's attendants are listening for. The structure is precise.

This is what the eleventh hour does. It orders the territory. It opens the gates in sequence. It cannot be hurried.

(pause)

If you have woken into this meditation briefly — if you are in the half-waking that sometimes occurs in the last stretch of sleep — let the body remain where it is. The eleventh hour can be inhabited consciously. The slowness in the body, the heaviness, the sense that you are about to wake but have not yet — these are the eleventh hour's quality. You are present in the preparation.

(pause)

There is one more work of this hour that the meditation needs to acknowledge.

The gods of the eleventh hour speak to the inhabitants of the regions the barque crossed. The dead of the third hour. The *bau* of Wernes. The chamber-gods of the eighth hour. The figures fed in the ninth. The regenerating bodies of the tenth. They are being told that the barque is leaving, that the dawn approaches, that the cycle is completing.

This is farewell.

(longer pause)

If a quiet melancholy is present in you now — a sadness without object, a grief without content, the strange quality of leaving that arrives sometimes in the last sleep before waking — let it be what it is.

The night that worked on you is ending. The territories that carried specific work are being released. The barque is leaving regions where labor was done on your behalf. The leaving has its quality, and the quality is registering.

This is not failure. This is not unprocessed material. This is the eleventh hour's farewell registering at the surface of awareness. Acknowledging it is sufficient. The territories will not be returned to in the same form until the next dusk opens them again. The leaving is real.

(pause)

Let the farewell occur.

You do not need to do anything to perform it. The gods of the eleventh hour are speaking the addresses to the inhabitants. The territory is being notified. The work is happening in you without requiring your direction. What is asked of you is the permission to feel what is being felt — the quiet grief that is the structural occurrence of the eleventh hour — and not to interpret it as wrongness.

(longer pause)

If you are in the longer eleventh hour of a season of your life — if you have come through a major passage and are now preparing to return to the daily life in your gathered form — let this meditation address that season as well.

The territories of the longer passage are being released. The dissolution that occurred over months. The defense that was sustained across weeks. The gathering that has finally completed. These are not coming with you in the same form into the living hours that are about to resume. What is coming with you is the gathered form. The territories themselves are being released.

The grief that arrives in the period before return is the farewell to those territories. Allow it. Do not rush past it. The eleventh hour cannot be skipped at the scale of a night or at the scale of a season. The dawn requires this hour. The return requires this farewell.

(pause)

What is being assembled in you now is the final shape of the form that will emerge at the dawn. The shaping serpent is completing its work. The gates are opening in sequence. The defeated of the night are being sorted into their containment. The dead are being told the cycle completes.

When the final gate opens — the gate that gives onto the eastern horizon — the eleventh hour will end. The twelfth will begin. But that is not yet. The eleventh is still doing its work.

(pause)

Let yourself remain present in the preparation. Do not lean forward into the dawn. The dawn will arrive when the dawn arrives. What is occurring now is the territory being ordered, the gates being opened, the farewell being performed. This is what the eleventh hour is.

You are nearly at the threshold.

The barque is approaching the final gate.

(longer pause)

What remains in you is only your weight, your breath, the dark that is beginning to lighten behind your closed eyes — or has not yet begun to lighten, depending on where you are in the actual hour of your night.

Either is correct. The eleventh hour does not require precise correspondence with the clock. It is the territory of preparation, and the territory is present whenever the preparation is occurring.

Rest now.

The gates are opening.

The Twelfth Hour

The eastern horizon. The crossing. The emergence as becoming.

What the Amduat Describes

The final gate of the eleventh hour opens. The Mesektet, carrying the renewed form, passes through and enters the territory of the twelfth hour — the cavern of the eastern horizon. This is the last region of the Duat. Beyond it is the threshold of the visible world.

The territory is depicted in the *Amduat* as a long, narrow passage. The walls of the chamber rise steeply on either side. At the far end is a figure: the double sphinx, sometimes called Aker, the lion-bodied god of the horizons. Aker's body is the structural threshold between the Duat and the daylight world. The barque must pass through Aker's body to complete the crossing.

The passage through Aker is the final transformation.

Ra enters as the diminished form that has been gathered and shaped across the deeper hours. Ra emerges from the other end of Aker's body as Khepri — the scarab-form of the rising sun, the god of becoming, the form that the entire night's labor has produced. The *Amduat* depicts this transformation with a specific image: the scarab appears at the far end of Aker, pushing the disk of the sun before it, in the act of emerging.

Khepri's name means *he who is coming into being*. This matters for what the twelfth hour actually depicts. The emergence is not the arrival of a static deity. It is the appearance of a form that is in the act of becoming what it will be. Khepri is not Ra-restored. Khepri is the dawn-god as motion — as the sun in the moment of arriving, not yet at midday, not yet at any subsequent position, but in the becoming that the dawn itself is.

At the moment of crossing, a second event occurs. The Mesektet remains behind. The Night Barque does not cross into the daylight world. It stays at the threshold of the eastern horizon, in the position it will hold throughout the day, waiting for the next dusk when it will receive Ra again at the western horizon.

Khepri boards a different vessel: the **Mandjet**, the Day Barque, which has been waiting at the eastern horizon. The vessel change mirrors the vessel change at dusk, but in reverse. At dusk, Ra left the Mandjet and boarded the Mesektet for the night journey. At dawn, Khepri leaves the Mesektet and boards the Mandjet for the day journey. The two vessels meet only at the thresholds. Each carries the god through the territory suited to its form.

The crew of the Mesektet — Hu, Sia, Heka, Wepwawet, the steersman — remains on the Night Barque. They have completed their function for this passage. They are not destroyed; they wait. The defenders likewise. Set, Mehen, Isis, Nephthys, Selket — all are released from active duty until the next passage requires them.

A different crew receives Khepri on the Mandjet. The day-crew, whose function is the carrying of the sun through the living hours. The *Amduat* does not describe this crew at the level of detail it gave to the night-crew, because the *Amduat* is the text of the night journey, not the day. The day-crew's work is not the subject of this passage. What the twelfth hour shows is the transfer: Khepri leaves one vessel and boards the other. The crossing is complete.

The inhabitants of the Duat have been told the cycle completes. They return to their permanent functions. The dead resume their stations in the field of Hour III. The *bau* of Wernes resume the territory they inhabit. The chamber-gods of the eighth hour return to their chambers. The provision-gods of the ninth, the regenerating gods of the tenth, the gate-attendants of the eleventh — all return to the positions they hold between passages. The Duat itself becomes quiet. The territory rests.

The twelfth hour ends with Khepri rising. The Mandjet begins its journey across the sky. The eastern horizon recedes behind the day-barque. The passage of the Duat is complete. The next dusk will begin the next passage, with the same structure, the same crew, the same defenders, the same gathering and shaping and emergence. But until then — for the duration of the living hours — the Duat is at rest.

The Theological Claim

The twelfth hour establishes the final claim of the entire passage: **the form that arrives at dawn is the form the passage produced, and the practitioner carries that form into the living hours.**

This is the consummation of everything the previous chapters built. The vessel change at dusk required a different form for the night. The merging at the still center dissolved that form. The meeting in the deep waters began reconstitution. The defense preserved what was reconstituting. The chambers received it. The provisions sustained the work. The gathering assembled the form. The shaping completed it. The gates released it. The crossing transforms it.

What emerges at the eastern horizon is the form that this entire labor produced. It is not the form the practitioner had at the previous dusk. It is the gathered, defended, received, provisioned, assembled, shaped, released, and transformed form — the form the passage made.

This is what the practitioner carries into the living hours.

Khepri's name carries the specific theological weight: *coming into being*. The form that emerges at dawn is not static. It is in the act of becoming what the day will make of it. The living hours that follow are not the resting state of the dawn-form; they are the territory in which the dawn-form continues to develop into what the day produces. The practitioner who wakes is not arriving at completion; the practitioner who wakes is beginning a different stage of the same becoming that the night performed.

This collapses a distinction that contemporary frameworks have been making since the practitioner began reading. The night and the day are not separate works. They are continuous. The passage of the Duat produces the form that enters the day. The day works on that form through its own labor — Helios's arc, the encounters of the living hours, the demands of the manifest world. At the next dusk, the form the day produced will be what enters the next night's Duat. The cycle continues. The becoming continues.

There is no completion in the sense of a final state. There is only the continuation of the becoming, hour by hour, day by day, passage by passage. Khepri is the name of this continuation. The dawn-form is the becoming-form.

The implication for the practitioner is the deepest claim the book has been building toward: **you are always in motion. The form you carry is always being made.**

The practitioner who has read this far has been operating, perhaps without naming it, on an assumption that healing or growth or arrival is a destination. The contemporary frameworks reinforce this. *You will reach a point. You will arrive. You will be done with the difficult passage and resume the ordinary life as a completed self.* The barque tradition does not promise this. The barque tradition promises something different and harder: the becoming does not end. The form is always being made. Every dawn is the emergence of a new form, and every dusk is the dissolution of that form into the next night's labor.

This is not bleak. This is the structure of the cosmology, and the cosmology is reliable. The becoming is sustained by structures that have been doing this work since before the practitioner was born and will continue doing it after the practitioner has died. The Mesektet carries every nightly passage. The Mandjet carries every daily one. The crew and defenders attend at every cycle. The gathering occurs at every tenth hour. The emergence completes at every twelfth.

What the practitioner is asked to do is what they have always been asked to do: consent to the passage. Board the Mesektet at dusk. Cross the night. Emerge as Khepri at dawn. Enter the living hours in the form the night produced. Cross those hours awake. Return to the threshold at dusk. Begin again.

This is what a life is, in the barque tradition's account. Not a series of arrivals at destinations, but the continuous becoming of a form that the daily passage produces. The practitioner is not building toward completion. The practitioner is participating in a cycle whose structure is reliable and whose work is continuous.

For the longer arc — for the practitioner who has been through a major life passage and has reached the equivalent of the twelfth hour of that longer arc — the claim is most demanding. The dawn that arrives after a longer dissolution is not the end of the passage in the sense of arriving at a finished state. It is the emergence of the form the longer passage produced, and that form is now beginning the next stage of its becoming. The practitioner who has come through grief or illness or vocational collapse and who is now structurally ready to resume the daily life in their gathered form is not done. They are emerging. The emergence is itself motion. The new form will continue to develop in the living hours that follow.

This is sometimes received with disappointment. The practitioner who has hoped for completion — *finally I will be on the other side of this, finally I will be done with the work the passage required* — meets the twelfth hour's claim and feels its weight. The completion they hoped for does not exist as the cosmology describes it. What exists is the continuation of the becoming.

The relief in this claim, properly understood, is the relief of structure. The becoming does not require the practitioner to direct it. The structures that produced the form at this dawn will produce the next form at the next dawn. The practitioner who wakes in the gathered form is not now responsible for maintaining that form against dissolution. The next dusk will come. The next Mesektet will receive them. The next passage will perform its work. The practitioner's job is what it has always been: to consent to the crossing.

The Crossing

The Mesektet approaches the body of Aker. The crew prepares for the threshold. Hu is silent; the speaking that has carried the passage through twelve hours is complete. Sia perceives the eastern horizon and what waits beyond it. Heka holds the assembled form in its functional integrity for the final crossing. Wepwawet stands at the prow; his work of opening the way has reached its final gate. The steersman holds the tiller for the last stretch.

The defenders are at rest. Set's spear is set aside. Mehen has uncoiled from the cabin. The protection is no longer needed; the cabin is opening. Ra in his diminished form is about to leave the cabin entirely.

The barque enters Aker's body. The passage through is brief in the *Amduat*'s depiction — a single image showing the barque inside the body of the double sphinx, in the moment of crossing. There is no narrative of the passage's interior. The threshold is not a place where time is reckoned. It is the point of transformation, and the transformation happens in the crossing itself.

The barque emerges from Aker. The form that emerges is no longer Ra in his diminished, gathered, shaped form. The form is Khepri. The transformation completed in the crossing. The scarab pushes the disk of the sun. The dawn is arriving.

At this moment the vessel change occurs. Khepri leaves the Mesektet. The Night Barque holds its position at the threshold. Khepri boards the Mandjet. The Day Barque receives him. The day-crew, whose work begins now, takes its stations.

The first light enters the world. The horizon is crossed. The living hours begin.

What This Means for the Practitioner

The twelfth hour is the structural location of the Dawn Rite that the original foundational chapters established. The rite is the practitioner's conscious participation in the crossing.

The rite acknowledges that the passage has occurred. The form that the practitioner inhabits in the morning is the form the passage produced. The Mesektet is behind. The Mandjet is here. The day is beginning. The practitioner is on the Day Barque now.

What the rite does not do — what the rite has never done — is claim that the practitioner has fully grasped what the passage performed. The deeper hours remain inaccessible to the conscious mind. The merging at the still center cannot be witnessed. The defense at the seventh hour cannot be observed. The gathering at the tenth hour cannot be tracked. The practitioner who performs the Dawn Rite is acknowledging the work without claiming to have seen it.

This is sufficient. The cosmology does not require the practitioner to witness what was done. The cosmology requires the practitioner to consent to the crossing and to receive what the crossing produced. The Dawn Rite is the structural form of that reception.

For the practitioner who has now read the entire arc of Hours of the Duat material, the twelfth hour completes the framework. You know, in cosmological terms, what the night does. You know who works the passage. You know what the territory contains. You know how the gathering occurs. You know what the dawn delivers.

What you do with this knowledge is not specified by the cosmology. The cosmology gives you the structure. The application is yours.

What can be said is what has been said across the chapters: the framework is available. The night does its work whether you witness it or not. The dawn arrives whether you have understood it or not. What changes when the framework is held is the practitioner's relationship to the passage, not the passage itself.

A practitioner who knows the structure of the night may cross it differently. Not more efficiently — the passage cannot be accelerated. Not more deeply — the depth is determined by the territory, not by the practitioner's awareness. What changes is the quality of the consent. The practitioner who knows the structure can consent more completely, with fewer reservations, with more trust in what has been built to carry them. The Mesektet has been receiving every practitioner who has ever slept. The defense has been holding every difficult night. The gathering has been occurring every tenth hour. The dawn has been arriving every twelfth.

You are not the first to make this passage. You will not be the last. What carries you tonight has carried every practitioner who has ever consented to the crossing. The cosmology is older than any framework you might bring to it, and it will outlast the frameworks that follow yours.

For the longer arc — for the season of a life that has been through a major passage and that is now structurally arriving at its own twelfth hour — the claim is the same and the implication is the same. The form you carry forward is the form the passage produced. You are not arriving at completion. You are emerging. The emergence will continue into the next stage of the becoming. The next dusk of the longer arc will eventually come. Another passage will begin.

This is not a burden. This is the structure of being alive. The practitioner who has come through one major passage will, in time, encounter another. The cosmology that carried them through this one will carry them through the next. The Mesektet does not run out of capacity. The crew does not flag. The defenders do not abandon. The gathering does not fail.

What you have is the framework, and the framework is enough.

A Practice for the Crossing

This final meditation is for use at the threshold of the dawn — for the practitioner who is preparing to wake, or who has just woken, or who is performing the Dawn Rite in conjunction with this material. It is shorter than the previous meditations because the twelfth hour does not require elaborate inhabitation; it requires only the acknowledgment of the crossing.

The eleventh hour is behind you. The gates have opened. The shaping is complete. The farewells have been performed.

(pause)

The Mesektet approaches the eastern horizon. Ahead is the body of Aker, the double sphinx of the threshold. Beyond Aker is the visible world.

You are at the crossing.

(pause)

The barque enters Aker's body. The threshold is brief. The transformation occurs in the crossing itself.

You emerge as Khepri.

(longer pause)

The form you carry now is the form the passage produced. It is not the form you had at the previous dusk. It is the gathered, defended, received, provisioned, assembled, shaped form — the form the entire night made.

This form is in motion. Khepri is the god of becoming. The dawn is not arrival at completion; the dawn is the beginning of the next stage of the be-coming.

(pause)

The Mesektet remains at the threshold. The Night Barque has done its work. The crew is at rest until the next dusk. The defenders are at rest. The inhabitants of the Duat have been told the cycle completes. The territory is quiet.

You are no longer on the Mesektet.

The Mandjet is waiting. The Day Barque receives you. The day-crew, whose work begins now, takes its stations.

(pause)

The first light enters the world. The horizon is crossed. The living hours begin.

(longer pause)

You do not need to remember what occurred in the deeper hours. The merging cannot be witnessed. The defense cannot be observed. The gathering cannot be tracked. What you carry is the result, not the record.

What you carry is sufficient.

The form is in motion. The day is beginning. The Mandjet is moving across the sky. The work of the living hours is the next stage of the becoming.

(pause)

Stand at the threshold for as long as the threshold remains available. The window is brief. Before the day's demands assemble themselves and claim your attention entirely, there is a moment when the night's communication is close to the surface and the form you carry is freshly emerged from the passage.

Meet the moment.

Then enter the living hours.

The Mesektet will be waiting at the next dusk. The crew will receive you again. The defenders will engage as the passage requires. The gathering will occur. The emergence will complete.

You will be carried as you have always been carried.

Rest now is no longer what is asked.

What is asked is what was asked at the threshold at dusk: cross awake.

The Map

A consolidated reference for the structure of the passage. The full map, with its seven strokes and threshold prompts, is in the Hours Companion Workbook.

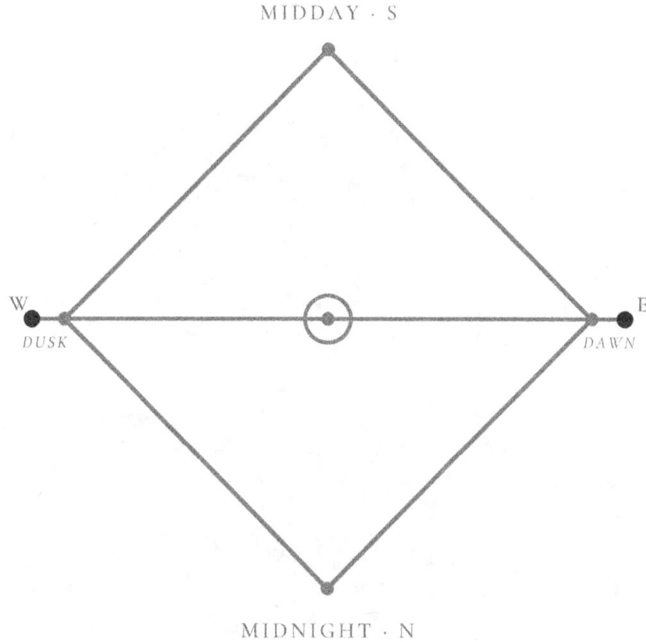

The Glyph

The glyph of Hours is a diamond bisected by a horizontal line. The diamond is the daily passage — the full arc from dusk through the night to dawn and the living hours beyond. The horizontal line is the threshold of waking, dividing what is seen from what is worked. The point at the center is the practitioner. Above is the day. Below is the night. The four cardinal points of the diamond are the four thresholds of the practice.

The Four Directions

Each direction holds an element, a time, and a presiding power. The logic is cosmological, not arbitrary — the eastern horizon is where Ra rises and therefore where the passage ends and the day begins; the western horizon is where the sun crosses into the Duat and Nyx takes her territory; the southern apex is the full arc of

Helios at midday; the northern depth is Osiris in his tomb at the fifth hour, the still center of the night.

Direction	Element	Time	Presence
East	Air	Dawn	Ra / Khepri
South	Fire	Midday	Helios
West	Water	Dusk	Nyx
North	Earth	Midnight	Osiris

The Practitioner at Center

The practitioner stands at the center of the glyph because the passage is always personal. The day moves around you and through you; you are not outside it looking in. The center is not a position of mastery. It is the position of presence — the only point from which the four directions can be held simultaneously. You are not crossing the diamond. You are the axis around which it turns.

Each of the four points asks a different quality of attention. At dusk, release. At midnight, consent. At dawn, reception. At midday, the apex — knowing where you are on the arc. These four movements are the daily practice that the Rites of the Hours library formalize.

The Body as Glyph

The three-point gesture is the glyph drawn in the body. You become what the symbol names.

Register Discernment

The Rites of Hours are written in three registers, formalized in the Hours Companion Workbook. They are not hierarchy. They are three valid doors into the same practice. This page describes each so you can recognize which voice is yours.

Acknowledgment

Acknowledgment is the register that names what is cosmologically true. It does not address the forces of the passage — it describes them. *Ra rises in the east. The threshold of dusk is open. Nyx holds the western horizon.* The practitioner speaks what is, and in speaking places themselves inside a structure that is already operating. Acknowledgment is theologically complete. It is not a provisional register for practitioners who have not yet developed devotional relationships; it is its own register, with its own integrity. What it offers is orientation without familiarity. The deities are present in the rite, but they are not being spoken to. They are being spoken of, the way one speaks of the north star — as a fact of the sky that locates the one standing beneath it.

Devotional

Devotional register changes the direction of the language. Where acknowledgment speaks *about* the deities, devotion speaks *to* them. *Nyx, you stand at the western threshold. Osiris, you hold what will be worked tonight.* This shift is not cosmetic. Direct address assumes relationship — that the deity is a person, not a principle, and that the practitioner has standing to address them. Devotional language works when the relationship already exists. It cannot be manufactured by changing pronouns. If the relationship is present, the devotional register adds a dimension that acknowledgment cannot reach: the practitioner is not only oriented within the structure, they are in conversation with the intelligence that governs it.

Non-deity

Non-deity register strips the names and speaks only of the elements and directions. *In the west, water. The threshold of dusk. The deep world opens.* This is not a register for practitioners who are uncomfortable with deity language — treating it that way underestimates what it does. Non-deity framing accesses something the other two registers, by naming specific deities, foreclose: the forces themselves, prior to personification. It is the register closest to the mechanics of the passage. Some days the deity language will feel like borrowed weight. On those days, non-deity language does not remove depth — it returns the practitioner to the structure beneath the names.

Which Is Yours

Most practitioners move between registers. The register that is yours on a given day is the one that lets you meet the threshold honestly. The full rite cards in all three registers — for each of the four thresholds — are in the *Hours Companion Workbook*.

The *Amduat* and its companion literature are attested across many royal tombs of the New Kingdom and have been studied for more than a century. Readers who wish to engage the primary sources and the scholarly literature on the Egyptian and Greek frames invoked across these chapters may find the following works useful starting points.

Assmann, Jan. *Death and Salvation in Ancient Egypt.* Translated by David Lorton. Ithaca: Cornell University Press, 2005.

Faulkner, R. O., trans. *The Ancient Egyptian Book of the Dead.* Edited by Carol Andrews. London: British Museum Press, 1985.

Hesiod. *Theogony, Works and Days, Testimonia.* Translated by Glenn W. Most. Loeb Classical Library. Cambridge, MA: Harvard University Press, 2006.

Homer. *The Iliad.* Translated by Robert Fagles. New York: Penguin Classics, 1990. Book XIV for the encounter of Hypnos and Nyx.

Hornung, Erik. *The Ancient Egyptian Books of the Afterlife.* Translated by David Lorton. Ithaca: Cornell University Press, 1999.

Hornung, Erik. *The Egyptian Amduat: The Book of the Hidden Chamber.* Translated by David Warburton. Zurich: Living Human Heritage Publications, 2007.

Schweizer, Andreas. *The Sungod's Journey through the Netherworld: Reading the Ancient Egyptian Amduat.* Translated by David Lorton. Ithaca: Cornell University Press, 2010.

Wilkinson, Richard H. *The Complete Gods and Goddesses of Ancient Egypt.* London: Thames & Hudson, 2003.

Hours is being written as a four-volume work. Volume I, *The Egyptian Passage*, is what you have just read — the cosmological foundation and the twelve hours of the Duat. Three volumes follow.

Volume II — Nyx's Household. The Greek night and its inhabitants. Nyx herself, older than the Olympian order. Hypnos and Thanatos. The Oneiroi who come through the gates of horn and ivory. The Moirai who spin and measure and cut. The river Lethe. The deities of sleep, dream, fate, and death who keep the dark hours, considered in the same depth that Volume I gives the Egyptian frame.

Volume III — The Otherworld. The Celtic deepening. The festival-cycle theology — Samhain, Imbolc, Beltane, Lughnasadh — and the otherworld geography that runs parallel to the visible world. The thin places. The sídhe. The hill and the dark. How the daily passage opens into the larger turn of the year.

Volume IV — Helios. The solar arc and the living hours. The day-work that is the necessary counterweight to the night-work. Where Volumes I through III move into the dark, Volume IV moves into the light — the chariot's crossing, the apex at midday, what the living hours actually require of the practitioner who has been carried through the Duat.

Each volume stands on its own. Together they map the night and the day across the traditions that took both most seriously.

Hours is the theology. The practice has its own home.

The *Hours Companion Workbook* is where the framework becomes a daily practice. It contains the four threshold rites — Dusk, Midnight, Dawn, Midday — in all three registers, with abbreviated forms for the days when the full rite is not possible. It contains the Map of the passage and the four directions. It contains threshold journals for each of the four crossings, check-ins for the first week and first month of the practice, and the work of register discernment as the practitioner moves through it.

The book is the framework. The workbook is the practice. Together they are what a daily theology actually looks like when you are inside one.

The workbook is available at:

gristtheology.com

If this book found you at a threshold, cross it.